The sweet taste of providence

God is at work throughout history, and Christine Farenhorst's fascinating vignettes are like little windows opening into a "vast cloud of witnesses." Readers will be challenged and encouraged!
—JANIE B. CHEANEY, senior writer, *WORLD* magazine, USA

Delightful, God-glorifying stories and thought-provoking questions —a helpful book for children and for adults as well. This sweet book is well-suited to move the mind and soul Godward through historical vignettes.
—JOEL R. BEEKE, president, Puritan Reformed Theological Seminary, Grand Rapids, USA

The history of the church is rich with men and women who blazed a trail for God. Their devotion, commitment and service for the gospel of Jesus Christ is contagious. Christine Farenhorst has provided us with timely devotional thoughts as we survey God's hand of providence through the annuals of history. These devotions are rich in content and application, and will be welcomed by anyone interested in drawing closer to God by following the examples of those who have come before us.
— STEVEN J. LAWSON, president, OnePassion Ministries, Dallas, USA

Who would not anticipate a new book from Christine Farenhorst? I treasure her ministry—a gift of God to the church today, multi-talented, devout, creative (see her happy crossword puzzles), four-square with a rich grasp of the history of the kingdom of God. Readers are in for a treat, certainly not a mere dutiful read.
—GEOFFREY THOMAS, pastor, Aberystwyth, Wales, UK

John Flavel, the English Puritan, said that life is like a Hebrew sentence; it is only rightly understood when read backwards. As we look back in history, whether our own or more broadly, we are able to see God's providential dealings with men. Christine Farenhorst reads backwards for us in these delightful vignettes taken from secular and church history. She gives us scriptural context for their consideration and questions for their discussion. This will be a helpful work for parents, teachers, pastors and all those who want to learn to delight in *The Sweet Taste of Providence*.
—JEFF KINGSWOOD, pastor, Grace Presbyterian Church (ARP), Woodstock, Ontario, Canada

The SWEET TASTE *of* PROVIDENCE

74 devotional episodes from history

CHRISTINE FARENHORST

joshua press

www.joshuapress.com

Publisher Joshua Press Inc., Kitchener, Ontario, Canada
Distributor Sola Scriptura Ministries International | **www.sola-scriptura.ca**

Cover and book design Janice Van Eck

Library and Archives Canada Cataloguing in Publication

Farenhorst, Christine, 1948–, author
    The sweet taste of providence : 74 devotional episodes from history
/ Christine Farenhorst.

Issued in print and electronic formats.
**ISBN 978-1-894400-71-8 (paperback).—ISBN 978-1-894400-72-5 (epub).
—ISBN 978-1-894400-73-2 (mobi)**

1. History—Religious aspects—Christianity. I. Title.

BR115.H5F37 2016   231.7'6   C2016-901929-2
                                                                 C2016-901930-6

Dedicated to my youngest son, Benjamin Anthony Louis,
who is truly a son of my right hand, and a son of happiness.

> *My son, eat honey, for it is good,*
> *and the drippings of the honeycomb*
> *are sweet to your taste,*
> *Know that wisdom is such to your soul;*
> *if you find it, there will be a future,*
> *and your hope will not be cut off.*
> *—Proverbs 24:13–14*

Contents

Devotional
for MT or
for OT

Introduction

t is incumbent upon parents to continually teach their children to discern and for teachers to diligently show their pupils the wonderful works of God. This is pursuing the injunction of Deuteronomy 6:7–9 where we read that the commandments of the Lord should be imprinted on hearts:

You shall teach them diligently to your children, and shall talk of them when you sit in your house, and when you walk by the way, and when you lie down, and when you rise. You shall bind them as a sign on your hand, and they shall be as frontlets between your eyes. You shall write them on the doorposts of your house and on your gates.

There are many distractions to attract and entice hearts away from the Lord's commandments in the twenty-first century. To this end, I hope that the power, majesty and providence of God clearly reflected in these short devotional stories and historical vignettes, will draw hearts to seek the face of God and motivate readers to praise his Name.

It is my prayer that those who read this volume will come away enriched and encouraged in the knowledge that their daily lives are totally within the scheme of God's perfect plan for them and that they will also diligently desire to fulfil Christ's great commission to make disciples of all nations.

01

Proverbs 20:15 *There is gold and abundance of costly stones,*
But the lips of knowledge are a precious jewel.

A precious jewel of a man

William Guthrie was born almost 400 years ago near Brechin, Forfarshire, Scotland.

"A fine bairn," his mother crooned as she held him in her arms and rocked him.

"A proper lad," his father agreed, as he leaned over her shoulder and looked at the small, red face of his first-born. For that is what William was—a firstborn child and very special in the eyes of his father and mother. They remarked on the baby's minuscule hands and feet and stroked the fine hair that covered his head, awed by the fact that this little child was their very own son. Then they prayed together, the father and the mother. They earnestly beseeched the Lord that their wee, red-faced William would grow up to serve his Father in heaven. Such prayers are good prayers, and they delight God who desires covenant parents to bring their children before him.

Father Guthrie was the owner of a fine estate called Pitforthy House. William, because he was the firstborn, was heir to this large house. But as the years passed and as he grew from baby to child to man, William became more and more certain that he was called, not to the task of running an estate, but to the task of preaching the gospel. For this reason, he gave his inheritance of Pitforthy House, with all its wealth and easy living, to a younger brother and enrolled at St. Andrews University. Unencumbered by worldly goods, William's entire being was given over to serving the Lord.

William was a cheerful man who was devoted to his Creator with his whole heart. He loved preaching, he delighted in the beauty of creation and he could laugh heartily. In light of the fact that he believed that God always took care of him, had giving his Son to die for him, he daily lived in a happy frame of mind. Settling in the small town of Fenwick, Scotland, he married Agnes Campbell, a graceful girl and one who also revered the Lord.

Now at this time in history, Scotland's church, or *kirk* as it was called, was under siege. There were those who wanted to recognize an earthly king as head of the church, and there were those who would only recognize Christ as the head of the church. William Guthrie was of the last sort, and he refused to buckle down under the rules and regulations which had been imposed on the church by King Charles Stuart and his party. Worship, William believed, and rightly so, should be preserved according to the Word of God and not according to the word of the king, even though the king should be respected.

Next to preaching and speaking about his great love for God, William liked fishing. He knew all the fishing holes and often as he walked about visiting the people of his parish, he carried a pole over his shoulder so that he might cast in a line if he chanced to pass a good fishing spot. Many people who lived in and around Fenwick did not go to church. William considered all of them part of his responsibility, cheerfully striding six or seven miles for a visit. There were no proper roads, and the countryside was full of morasses. Here and there, people were rude enough to close a door in his face when he knocked, but he never gave up. Sometimes he disguised himself, often obtaining a night's lodging in a cottage which had previously refused him entrance. He always used the opportunity to speak of Christ and of eternal things.

Once meeting an elderly poacher out in the field, he struck up a conversation.

"I have my best sport," the man said proudly, "when others are in kirk. I can poach to my heart's content, and there is no one who will stop me, as the law is at worship."

William nodded and listened.

"Often on a Monday," the man went on boastfully, "I can earn a half a crown at market by selling the moorfowl and hares I have caught on Sunday."

"I will pay you a half-crown," William replied, "if you will come to kirk next Sabbath."

They shook hands on it, and William paid the man, who kept his bargain and came to kirk. Afterwards, William repeated his offer. But the Holy Spirit had done his work. There was no need to pay the old poacher. He came willingly from then on and, in time, was ordained as an elder.

Because God was gracious enough to bless William Guthrie's zeal for him, his parish became a well of water for all those thirsty to hear God's Word. People came from far and wide to hear the preaching, and God's kingdom grew. There is a saying that when you tread on the devil's tail, he squeals. The king's councillors, jealous of the Spirit's work in Fenwick, began to keep tabs on the congregation. They knew that William did not recognize the king as head of the kirk, that he did not implement the king's rules, and they hated him. In the summer of 1664, when William was thirty-four years old, twelve soldiers accompanied by a wicked curate, came to his house to tell him that he was being suspended from office and no longer allowed to preach. William and his wife received the officers graciously and asked them in.

"You have been shown great leniency so far," the curate said as he regarded William with dislike.

"I thank the Lord for that," William answered, "and I look upon it as a door which God opened to me for preaching the gospel."

The curate did not reply. William then turned to the twelve soldiers who stood uneasily in the front room of his home.

"As for you, gentlemen," he went on, "I wish the Lord may pardon you for countenancing this man in this business."

"I trust we may never do a worse thing," answered one of the rougher men, laughing as he said so.

"A little sin may damn a man's soul," responded William Guthrie, regarding the man keenly.

His wife came in with refreshments for the entire group and William asked a blessing on it. The persecuted then served the persecutors before the curate stood up to go out to tell the people waiting in the church next door that their pastor had been evicted from its pulpit.

Many pastors like William Guthrie were either hung or beheaded for preaching a gospel that only countenanced Christ as head of the church. William Guthrie, however, was not martyred. He died of natural causes, not too long after being taken out of the pulpit.

Food for thought

1. Can you think of people today who have been, or are, denied permission to speak out for the truth in God's Word? Have you yourself ever been ridiculed or stopped from saying something at school, work or anywhere else? If not, was that because you were afraid to speak up?

2. Was William Guthrie's success in preaching due to eloquence, love for people or Bible knowledge? Or, was it a combination of those things? Why or why not?

02

1 **Samuel 17:40** *Then he took his staff in his hand, and chose five smooth stones from the brook, and put them in his shepherd's pouch. His sling was in his hand, and he approached the Philistine.*

Drawing near to the Philistines

The story of David battling Goliath is a favourite one with both adults and children. Even unbelievers like the tale, comparing David to the underdog, the little man, who achieves victory over the impossible dictator. We have all placed ourselves, while reading this story or similar ones, in David's sandals. What would we have done? How would we have responded? Is there courage hidden within our hearts ready to come out at a moment's notice should we be confronted by an imposing, colossal Goliath?

These are good questions! These are essential questions—but

not questions one should ponder ahead of time. Jesus tells us, "Do not be anxious about your life, what you will eat or what you will drink, nor about your body, what you will put on. Is not life more than food and the body more than clothing? Look at the birds of the air" (Matthew 6:25–26). He goes on to say and point out as of primary importance, "Seek first the kingdom of God and his righteousness" (Matthew 6:33).

Emmi Delbrück was born in 1905, the second-youngest child in a family of seven in the Berlin suburb of Grunewald. She was nine when the First World War broke out. In 1930, she married Klaus Bonhöeffer (the famous Rev. Dietrich Bonhöeffer's brother). The 1930s were a tumultuous decade and held many Goliaths, as well as innumerable ordinary everyday Davids who had shepherds' bags. Later, when she was an old woman, Emmi was interviewed about the Nazi era. In her memories resided long-past anecdotes of people who had been Davids. Here is one of those stories.

An old, Christian German *hausfrau*, about ninety years of age, whose daughter and husband had become enamored by Hitler, was accustomed to order certain items from a Jewish shop. She bravely continued to do so after a boycott on Jewish shops had been imposed by the government. One day, as her daughter was visiting, some linen was delivered—linen her mother had ordered from a Jewish supplier.

"Mama," cried the enraged daughter, "I see you are still buying from the Jews. I'm afraid you must choose—either the Jews or me."

The old mother didn't even pause to swallow, but replied to her angry daughter in even tones, "My child, I choose the Jews."

Continuing to defy the boycott against Jews, this same old woman periodically bought a quarter-of-a-pound of butter at a certain dairy. Not too long after the incident with her daughter, a German officer wearing high, black polished boots, stood outside the Jewish shop as she was on her way in.

"Ho, grandmother," he addressed her, "are you sure you want to continue buying butter from a Jew?"

The old lady lifted her cane and smacked the officer on the toe of his polished boots so hard that he winced.

"I shall buy my butter where I have always bought it," she responded and walked into the store with her head held high.

Emmi Delbrück recounted another David story. At the end of 1941 she was on a crowded tram in the city of Kurfürstendamm. The tram made its usual stops, and at one of these an old Jewish lady got on—a lady with a conspicuous yellow star sewn onto the lapel of her coat. A man, an average everyday labourer, stood up in full view of everyone.

"Please," he addressed the Jewish woman in loud but good-tempered Berliner vernacular, "Please take my seat, my little shooting star."

The woman stood immobile, frozen in fear. The conductor lost no time in pushing his way past the people. Red in the face and puffed up with authority, he parked himself in front of the man.

"Surely you know that Jews are not allowed to sit down on trams."

The man smiled at him as if he, the conductor, was insane.

"Let me tell you something, mister. I decide for myself what happens to my behind."

Shoving the man and his misplaced authority aside, he walked toward the door and got out at the next stop. The woman cowered in front of the conductor. Emmi Delbrück, a professing Christian, was among the people on the crowded aisle on the bus. She nudged her way through and pushed the Jewish woman into the empty seat, whispering that she should stay there. The conductor said nothing and edged his way back to the front of the bus. Emmi then remained next to the woman until she had to get off.

Does it take a time of war to bring out the shepherds' bags? Surely not! Are there not Goliaths all around us today?

Food for thought

1. A woman at the check-out counter curses; a fellow-student repeatedly uses God's name in vain; and a neighbour swears when the snow-plow hits his mailbox. Are these Goliaths? Why or why not? How does God expect us to react?

2. There are issues, as well as people that rank highly with evil rulers who profane and insult God. How could the issue of marriage, for

example, become a mockery and insult God? Or, how do you handle conversation with a friend whose mother is suffering from Lou Gehrig's disease (ALS) and wants "death with dignity"—a "physician assisted" suicide?

03

Genesis 12:1–4 *Now the Lord said to Abram, "Go from your country and your kindred and your father's house to the land that I will show you. And I will make of you a great nation, and I will bless you and make your name great, so that you will be a blessing. I will bless those who bless you, and him who dishonors you I will curse, and in you all the families of the earth shall be blessed." So Abram went, as the Lord had told him.*

Go to the land I will show you

In 1870, a church was built in a very poor district of Liverpool, England. As a matter of fact, the district was so poor, it was known as "the little hell." The houses were small; the streets smelled and were filled with refuse; drunkards, both men and women, generally lay lolling in the gutters, and half-naked children ran about with no one to care for them.

The church, which was named Nathaniel Church, was built of grey brick and could hold 750 people. There were those who laughed at the church's size and said that surely the pews would never be filled. They believed the drunkards, guttersnipes and thieves of the alleys could never be induced to sit inside a sanctuary. But Richard Hobson, the minister of Nathaniel Church, was not discouraged. He made friends with the little children on the street and visited all the people in the neighbourhood.

True love shown in the name of the Lord Jesus Christ is a wonderful thing. Before too many months had passed, people began attending Nathaniel Church. They were poor people who, although they did not have Sunday clothes, did have open ears and open hearts.

Richard Hobson did not earn a big salary. As a matter of fact, he had very little to call his own. One day, two strangers attended Nathaniel Church. Well-dressed men, they approached Rev. Hobson after the service.

"We liked your preaching," one of them said with a smile as he shook Rev. Hobson's hand.

"We liked it so much," the other added, "that we would like to offer you another post—the post of Holy Trinity Church in Runcorn."

Richard Hobson stared at them. He knew the church they were talking about and could clearly visualize it in his mind's eye. It was a large church with schools built next to it. He was also aware that there was an associate pastor to help with the work.

"The manse, the house you will be given in which to live," the first man added, "is roomy and comfortable, and your salary will be £300 a year.

That's ten times as much as I am earning right now in Nathaniel Church. The thought flashed through Richard's mind before he could help it, and he closed his eyes for a moment.

"I'll think on it," he told the gentlemen, and they left after shaking his hand once more and commenting again on just how much they had liked his sermon.

The proposal the men had made to Richard Hobson was generous. Many of his friends believed it was a direct call from God. They said that such a wonderful offer could not be refused. Richard Hobson, however, was not so sure. He was tempted by the comfortable house, the decent wage and the well-established church. But on the other hand, he saw the hunger and the need for God's Word in the eyes of the poor in his neighbourhood. He wrote down the reasons why he wanted to leave and the reasons why he wanted to stay on a piece of paper. Then he knelt down on the floor and prayed. There was no doubt in his mind after his prayer that God had spoken to him, saying, "Richard Hobson, you have left the comforts of your home to come to this filthy neighbourhood because I have called you to come here, and here you should stay. Do not be tempted by material goods. Let the people here be blessed by the message you will give about me."

One day, shortly after his decision, a young girl was shown into Richard Hobson's study. She was nervous and afraid, twisting her hands as she stood in front of his desk.

"I have come to tell you that I am so glad that you will stay here."

"Please sit down," Rev. Hobson said.

The girl was about to take a seat across from him. But, before doing so, she reached into a torn pocket and pulled out a bankbook. This she handed to Rev. Hobson as she smiled timidly. Then she sat down, words tumbling out across the desk as she took her seat.

"Please take this, sir. As a thank offering to God, I wish you to take for your use whatever is in my book. I have not saved much money, but I want you to have it all."

When Rev. Hobson shook his head and moved the book across the desk back to her, she put her face into her hands and began to cry.

"I'm sorry. I know it's not very much...."

"Why, exactly," Rev. Hobson asked kindly, "is it that you are making a thank offering?"

"Because only two months ago," the girl responded, drying her eyes with a scrap of cloth dug up from her pocket, "I went to Nathaniel's for the first time. And I heard you say things I had never heard before, and I went again and again. And now, sir," and she smiled again, "now I do believe I am a child of God. That is why I have brought you my savings. Because you are staying, and I will hear and learn more."

Rev. Hobson smiled also. He did not take the bankbook, but he felt God had confirmed him in his decision to stay by giving him a bonus worth much more than a salary of £300 a year.

Later in 1870, there was a smallpox epidemic in Liverpool. Although Richard Hobson knew the disease was very contagious, he visited throughout the neighbourhood as he had always done. One day, he was called to the home of a young Christian girl who was very ill. She was engaged to be married but was so sick there was very little hope of recovery. Her body was covered with scabs and her arms, full of sores, lay helpless on the sheets. As Rev. Hobson came in, her eyes lit up. She was so glad to see him. And that was not all. She lifted up her right hand, a hand oozing with pus, a hand that wanted to hold his. For a moment Rev. Hobson hesitated and recoiled within himself. But then he took her hand. She squeezed it and the pus ran down his fingers. The small room was crowded with people—a mother, a father as well as five other relatives. Rev. Hobson asked them to kneel with him in prayer. The dying girl held his hand firmly all the while and only when he said "Amen" did she let her grip loosen. Later her mother and father as well as a brother also came to know the Lord. The Holy Spirit had touched their hearts through the love shown by Richard Hobson, God's faithful servant—a love shown not only in words but also in deeds.

Richard Hobson served at the Nathaniel Church for thirty-three years, never leaving the position to which God had called him.

Food for thought

1. Would it have been wrong for Richard Hobson to leave Nathaniel Church? Had you been him, would you have left Nathaniel Church for the call to Runcorn? Why or why not?

2. Suppose yourself to be the girl who came to visit Richard Hobson in his study. How does her enthusiasm in giving compare to the Magi and their worship of Christ? How does your own enthusiasm and giving compare?

04

Proverbs 30:33
For pressing milk produces curds,
pressing the nose produces blood,
and pressing anger produces strife.

The Lion of the North

G ustavus Adolphus lived from 1594 to 1632. He was King of Sweden for twenty-one of those years (1611–1632), and was known by both those who loved him and those who hated him as, "The Lion of the North." Gustavus was born in Stockholm and was the grandson of Gustavus Vasa. (This grandfather, by the way, had made Lutheranism the state religion of Sweden in 1529.) As a child, Gustavus Adolphus was trained in military skills and tactics, and his understanding of warfare was remarkable. He inherited the throne of Sweden when he was only seventeen years old—not quite a child and not quite a man. However, because it was not just the throne he inherited but also three wars, he quickly became a man. His father, Charles IX, had been at war with Russia, Denmark and Poland.

Suffice it to say, young Gustavus acquitted himself well on the war front. There was somewhat of a David in him. He was a serious young man, a young man who loved the Lord God and who prayed much before coming to decisions. When fellow Protestants were threatened in 1630 by the Catholic League—whose army was commanded by a harsh commander named Tilly—young Gustavus Adolphus led a well-trained army of some 13,000 troops into Germany to come to their aid. Gustavus won a great victory with his Swedish soldiers. He died in battle two years later. A man of high moral character and of great piety, he was only thirty-eight years old.

Gustavus was much admired by his soldiers. They looked up to him. It was not because he had great physique or some sort of charisma that they were in awe of their commander. Rather, it was because of his humility—that outstanding trait which separates godly men from those who seek honour for themselves.

On one occasion, at a public review in Stockholm, before a battle was to take place, Gustavus had a quarrel with one of his officers, Colonel Seaton—an officer who was well-respected and who was highly competent. In a moment of anger, Gustavus struck this officer. Colonel Seaton was so humiliated and angered by his king's act, that he immediately went to his tent and wrote out his resignation. In it, he demanded an honourable discharge. After he wrote it, hands trembling and eyes aflame, he strode over to Gustavus' tent. Pushing the sentries aside, he glared at them.

"I have business with the king."

They let him pass and looked knowingly at one another. The matter that had happened at the public review was now common knowledge. The men whispered to one another, some siding with Gustavus and some with Seaton.

Inside the tent, without saying a word, Seaton walked up to Gustavus, handing him the paper in which he demanded his discharge. Gustavus took it from him, sat down and read it. He then asked Seaton if he was quite sure this was what he wanted.

"It is, sire," Seaton replied, looking him straight in the eye.

"Very well," Gustavus responded.

He stood up, walked over to his desk and signed the resignation. Handing the document back to Colonel Seaton, he sighed deeply.

"You may go."

Seaton bowed stiffly and left the tent.

After Colonel Seaton was gone, Gustavus sat down again. Many things went through his mind. Colonel Seaton had served him long and well. Turning back time was impossible, but if he could, perhaps he might not have dealt his trusted soldier that blow. It had been done without thinking. It had been an ill and unwise act. Gustavus prayed on the matter. He knew his Bible well and readily recalled the words of Proverbs 29:11, "A fool gives full vent to his spirit, but a wise man quietly holds it back," and he was ashamed.

"Your Majesty?"

It was one of his aides.

"Yes?"

"Your Majesty, Colonel Seaton intends to set out in the morning for Denmark."

"For Denmark?"

Denmark was not an ally. Rather, it was an enemy nation.

"Yes, your Majesty, for Denmark."

The next morning, even as Seaton rode off on his horse, Gustavus together with an officer and two grooms, followed him from afar. After having ridden quite a distance, they came to the Danish frontier. Gustavus told his companions, save one groomsman, to stay behind. He then began to gallop and overtook Seaton on a large plain. He rode next to his erstwhile colonel, speaking to the man as he did so.

"Dismount, sir! That you have been injured I acknowledge; I am, therefore, now come to give you the satisfaction of a gentleman. For being now out of my own dominions, we are equal. We have both, I see, pistols and swords. Alight, sir, immediately, and the affair shall be decided."

Seaton, after recovering from the total surprise of hearing what Gustavus had to say, dismounted from his horse, even as his sovereign had. But, after he dismounted, he did not reach for either his pistol or his sword. Instead he fell down on his knee.

"Sire," he said, "you have more than given me satisfaction, in condescending to make me your equal. God forbid that my sword should do any mischief to so brave and gracious a prince! Permit me to return to Stockholm and allow me the honour to live and die in your service."

The king, with tears in his eyes, raised up Colonel Seaton and embraced him. They returned to Stockholm as friends. When Gustavus and Seaton entered camp together, riding side by side, you can be sure that the entire camp was astonished at the turn of events.

Food for thought

1. If everyone were to pursue some friend or acquaintance who had some grievance against him, whether imagined or real, and made it known that he wanted to humble himself before that person so that friendship could be reestablished, what would the consequences be?

2. Jesus, who has never harmed us or treated us in any way unfairly, meets each of us on our road. How can we, practically speaking, dismount and kneel, and say to him that we would like to have the honour to live and die in his service?

05

Acts 27: 9–11; 14–15 *Since much time had passed, and the voyage was now dangerous because even the Fast was already over, Paul advised them, saying, "Sirs, I perceive that the voyage will be with injury and much loss, not only of the cargo and the ship, but also of our lives." But the centurion paid more attention to the pilot and to the owner of the ship than to what Paul said…But soon a tempestuous wind, called the northeaster, struck down from the land. And when the ship was caught and could not face the wind we gave way to it and were driven along.*

The lives of those who sailed
PART 1

On November 24, 1854, God commanded that some of the contents of his storehouses of snow be emptied on Southern Ontario, Canada. For it is so that when snow falls anywhere on earth, he has always ordered it. He also commanded the tempest to come out of its chamber to visit that same area. Consequently, cold driving winds churned up the water of Lake Erie, the southernmost of the Great Lakes. Black, icy waves crested high. Gale-force winds howled. It was, as they say, weather fit for neither man nor beast.

A merchant schooner, *The Conductor*, was sailing on Lake Erie that day. She was being tossed up and down like a toy boat. Her captain, Robert Hackett, tried to keep her on course. His heart pounded and leapt. He deeply rued the fact that he had insisted on sailing from Buffalo for Toronto that morning with his cargo of 10,000 bushels of wheat. He had thought he could beat the approaching storm, which he had known was gathering. Now, as he stood at the wheel, he gritted his teeth and relied on dead reckoning for his position. But God's breath hampered his vision and all eight crew members aboard the ship were in peril of their lives because of his faulty decision. He could see no familiar landmarks along the shore, when indeed he could see the shore. Around midnight, the three-masted vessel struck an outer sandbar off the south beach of Long Point. Even as the breakers lifted the boat, clearing her off the sandbar, she groaned, creaked and keeled over broadside into another sandbar. Water rushed over the deck, and she began to sink quickly.

The men, all eight of them, praying as they did so, scrambled for safety into the rigging.

"Tie yourselves tight, lads," Captain Hackett called out, as he climbed high with his crew, "and pray that the ship won't break up before daylight."

Lashing themselves to the rigging, all the men were soaked to the skin. Ice formed in their beards and crusted over their clothes. Shivering, they awaited morning. Their hopes were dashed as the faint morning light revealed their way out, the yawl boat, had been torn off the chocks and davits. There was no safe way to leave the sinking ship. The only passage to land was a swim through the cold and broad breakers smashing onto the beach.

On shore, not too far from where the ship was stranded, stood the Becker cabin. In the lee of a foredune, it had been built from the lumber of shipwrecked vessels. Inside its relative safety, twenty-three-year-old Abigail Becker woke early that morning from a troubled sleep. Her trapper husband, Jeremiah, was not home. She had heard the north-west wind blowing hard all night, keening like a mourner. Swinging her long legs over the edge of her bed, she stretched for a moment before stepping onto the wooden floor. Dressing warmly, she proceeded to build up the kitchen fire for breakfast. Then, wrapping herself in a shawl, Abigail left her five step-children in the cabin, together with the four little ones who were her own, and walked across the storm-swept beach to get a pail of water. She spotted *The Conductor* immediately. Its useless sails flapped loudly in the wind. She also saw the sailors strapped in the rigging. Wasting no time, she ran back to the cabin.

"Children," she began, as soon as she crossed the threshold, "there's a ship grounded about a mile up the beach. We must go and help, and we must hurry, or the poor sailors aboard will die."

Her children lost no time in getting dressed and helping their mother. They were used to the lake and to storms and had helped shipwrecked seamen before. One child collected blankets, another found matches, a third took the kettle, while the others ran outside to collect driftwood for a fire.

When the eight men in the rigging saw Abigail and her children coming across the sand dunes toward where they had run aground, they gave a cheer. They saw Abigail waving at them and stiffly taking their hands off the rigging, they returned her greeting. Straining their eyes, they observed her boys building a fire on the beach. Then they saw the woman motioning to them.

"She means for us to swim to shore," said one of the men, "but I'm not at all certain we'll make it."

Robert Hackett looked at his crew. He knew they would all be lost if they stayed strapped to the rigging. There was precious little chance another boat would come along to pick them up. He swallowed hard and then began taking off his greatcoat. Next, he kicked off his boots. His men watched him—watched him and the great stretch of water between them and the shore. But none dissuaded him from being the first to try for the safety of the beach.

"If we remain here," the captain spoke tersely, hands clenched on the rigging, "we are certain to die. On the other hand, with this woman's help, we may reach that fire we can all see burning. I will go first. If I get to shore safely, you will know to follow me one by one."

Hardly were the words out of his mouth before his men saw him plunge into the water. The waves carried him down water quite a distance. Abigail followed his progress along on land. Swimming strongly, the captain managed to gain footing closer to shore. But huge, breakers filled his mouth and eyes with sand and the undertow, treacherous and strong, began carrying him back into the deep. Abigail, who was a tall woman, waded into the water at this point. She caught Robert by the hand and pulled him to safety. Supporting him under the shoulder, she managed to walk him to the fire.

Food for thought

1. Was the captain responsible for the lives of his men? Are commanders of groups in a position of greater responsibility than others? Why or why not? Would you rather be a commander or one under authority?

2. Was Abigail obligated to help the men? Why or why not?

06

Acts 27:21–24 *Since they had been without food for a long time, Paul stood up among them and said, "Men, you should have listened to me and not have set sail from Crete and incurred this injury and loss. Yet now I urge you to take heart, for there will be no loss of life among you, but only of the ship. For this very night there stood before me an angel of the God to whom I belong and whom I worship, and he said, 'Do not be afraid, Paul; you must stand before Caesar. And behold, God has granted you all those who sail with you.'"*

The lives of those who sailed
PART 2

Abigail's children had put tea into the kettle and poured a steaming hot drink for the shivering captain. She left him in their care and ran back to the edge of the water, beckoning that a second man should brave the water.

One by one the men swam ashore, and one by one Abigail Becker, her long skirts sodden and wet, met them in the surf as they struggled against the hurtling strength of each new wave. Some appeared stronger and were able to walk to the fire; others were only half-conscious when they reached the shore and had to be heavily supported. Abigail took off her shawl and her shoes and put them on the men one at a time until she got them all to the house. The older children had stoked up the fire in the cabin, and it was burning lustily. There they stood, seven shivering souls, stretching out their hands to the flames. Their clothes were laid out on a drying rack of sorts and their money was spread out on the floor to dry. Beards dripped seawater. The children watched from a corner, and the seamen, relieved to be rescued from certain death, grinned at the little ones—remembering their own children whom, God willing, they should now see again.

There was, however, one man who would not risk the swimming, and he was still hanging in the rigging. No amount of gesturing and waving on Abigail's part could make him venture into the water. It was the cook—and he could not swim. As the storm continued and the wind howled on, everyone agreed that nothing more could be done for the fellow. The short winter day was ending, and the men, who together with Abigail had taken turns going out to look at the ship, now settled into the cabin for the night. They all slept heavily. Stress and cold had taken their toll. All, that is, but Abigail. She could not get the poor cook out of her mind, and she could see the poor fellow lashed to the rigging each time she closed her eyes.

Early the next morning, she was the first one up. Dressing quickly, she went outside. He who had cut the channel for torrents of rain and a path for the thunderstorm, had let the storm abate somewhat. It was much quieter. Abigail could see that the cook was still on the rigging. She strained her eyes and fancied that she could see him move. She went back inside. The men were stirring from their various places on the floor of the cabin. Feeding them breakfast, she suggested that there was enough wood on shore to build a raft, and they might be able to come alongside the schooner to help the cook to safety.

Enthusiastically, the crew went to work. They were able to construct a raft of sorts from the washed-up timber. They poled it out alongside the wreck of *The Conductor*. The cook's eyes were closed but he was still breathing. Somehow they managed to untie his cramped and frozen fingers from the rigging. He was more dead than alive. They brought him to shore, carried him into the cabin and Abigail put his frozen feet in cold water to draw out the frost.

Who is to say whether or not these men, plucked from the very jaws of death, pondered on the Almighty? It is known that they prayed. But even those who are not Christians have been known to pray. It is instinctive for a soul to call out to God, even if he has not professed belief previously. It is not known whether, as a result of their near-death experience, any of these eight men had a turnabout in their lives or a consequent walk with God.

Food for thought

1. Do you need faith in Jesus Christ in order to be able to pray? Why or why not?

2. Abigail Becker, who could neither swim nor write, received many honours because of the courage she displayed. She received a signed letter from Queen Victoria, as well as a medal from the United States government. Considering the Acts 27 passage, if you did something brave, by whom would you want to be recognized? Why?

07

Ecclesiastes 9:11–12 *Again I saw that under the sun the race is not to the swift, nor the battle to the strong, nor bread to the wise, nor riches to the intelligent, nor favor to those with knowledge, but time and chance happen to them all. For man does not know his time. Like fish that are taken in an evil net, and like birds that are caught in a snare, so the children of man are snared at an evil time, when it suddenly falls upon them.*

Arsenic and Waterloo

About 80 percent of all treated wood in Canada is treated with something called chromated copper arsenate, or CCA. This wood is used for projects such as backyard decks, fences, telephone and other utility poles—projects in which the ordinary Canadian is usually involved at least once in their life. The United States had phased out all such arsenic treated wood by 2003. In the spring of 2004, all such wood began to carry a warning label in Canada saying that it contained an arsenic-based preservative.

Arsenic is a toxic metal linked to cancer and CCA is an arsenic-laden pesticide that protects wood from insects and rot. There are alternatives, however, which can be used on wood to protect it from such things.

Napoleon Bonaparte died at the relatively young age of fifty-one on the island of St. Helena in 1821. There is no quibble about the fact that he died, but the cause of his death has been a puzzle for some 120 years. Suggestions as to the cause of his death have ranged from hepatitis, syphilis, malaria and poisoning to tuberculosis and cancer.

There are some undisputed facts as to his life. The most well-known of these facts are that he crowned himself Emperor of France in 1804 and, after ruling for ten years as virtual master of Europe, was defeated by the Englishman, the Duke of Wellington, at Waterloo in 1815. An undoubted military genius, who also possessed magnificent administrative ability, Napoleon ended up a defeated and lonely exile on the island of St. Helena.

St. Helena is an island, but it can actually be more accurately described as a hot and volcanic rock jutting out of the Atlantic Ocean, some 1,200 miles off the west coast of Africa. Consisting of forty-seven square miles, it was a lonely place. The single-story building constructed there for Napoleon and his French officers and servants was extremely damp. Initially during his captivity, Napoleon seems to have had a fairly free hand. He was permitted to go horseback riding and to do a bit of gardening.

However, as time went on, his captors deprived him of both his companions and his outdoor activities. Confined to Longwood House, the name of his residence, he became depressed. Lapsing into ill health, his symptoms included chills, nausea and fevers. His legs began to swell so that he was unable to walk without pain. He vomited from time to time and complained of headaches, lethargy and dizziness. His skin began to take on a yellowish tinge.

He would recuperate briefly, only to be overtaken by another bout of illness. Doctors attended him but confessed they were puzzled. Some called him a hypochondriac; others said he suffered from hepatitus. Eventually Napoleon, weak and extremely debilitated, was confined to the drab and very damp livingroom of Longwood House. There he slipped into a coma from which he never awoke.

The day after Napoleon died, May 6, 1821, an autopsy by a group of English doctors determined that the late Emperor of France had succumbed to a cancerous ulcer of the stomach. This greatly pleased the English, as it absolved them from any blame as to the cause of his death. At that time, cancer was considered a killer disease. Napoleon's father had died of it.

There have been many since that day in May 1821, however, who have hinted that the diagnosis made by the English physicians was a cover-up and that the symptoms exhibited by Napoleon were not compatible with cancer.

In 1961, Dr. Sten Forshufvud of Sweden first brought forth the theory that Napoleon actually died of arsenic poisoning. He came to this conclusion after analyzing a lock of Napoleon's hair. The hair contained high concentrations of arsenic. Arsenic was a fairly common ingredient in medicine and tonic preparations during Napoleon's time, and, given all the complaints that he had, he probably had his share of medicine. Dr. Forshufvud's discovery, therefore, did not lead to the conclusion that Napoleon had been poisoned.

Another later discovery, however, by a British chemist, David Jones, brought something else to light. In the late eighteenth and early nineteenth centuries, a type of pigment known as Scheele's green was commonly used to colour fabrics, paints and wallpapers. Guess what this pigment contained? It contained arsenic. This pigment was generally safe, or harmless, in fabrics and paint as long as they were on dry walls. In a damp environment though, Scheele's green would become moldy and arsenic would be released from the wallpaper in the form of a vapour. Whoever occupied a room with this type of wallpaper would literally be inhaling arsenic.

The wallpaper in Napoleon's livingroom had been preserved. A sample of it was taken to a laboratory to be tested. It was consequently found to contain a substantial amount of arsenic. Although it cannot be proven that Napoleon was poisoned by his wallpaper, it is certainly an interesting hypothesis in light of the fact that by 1900 Scheele's green had given symptoms of arsenic poisoning to hundreds of other people who had used wallpaper containing it in their homes.

So while industry is looking for an alternative to arsenic-based preservatives, perhaps it would be wise to think twice about building that new porch this summer. We all know that Napoleon met his Waterloo, but are we aware of what permanently decked him?

━━━━━━

Food for thought

1. The last sentence in this chapter might make you smile. But what is the answer to the question it poses? Prove your answer from the Bible.

2. Comment on Proverbs 21:1: "The king's heart is a stream of water in the hand of the Lord; he turns it wherever he will."

08

Proverbs 25:15 *With patience a ruler may be persuaded, and a soft tongue will break a bone.*

Aylmer's humble tooth

I t doesn't matter who you are—queen, prime minister or farmer —at some point you will get cavities. Sooner or later, all of us end up either with a permanent toothache or in a dentist's chair. The teeth we are born without and whose first cutting of is always hailed with so much excitement, can be the cause of a great deal of distress and pain.

Queen Elizabeth I (reigned 1558–1603), whose teeth lasted a lot shorter time period than her illustrious reign, did not use a wooden toothpick. She owned and used several sets of gold toothpicks, which she kept in a jewel-encrusted case.

Queen Elizabeth I is rarely, if ever, seen smiling in portraits. She had unhealthy teeth. It was no help that she owned gowns of gold cloth, richly embroidered mantles, a salt-shaker made of mother-of-pearl, innumerable jewels, silver fans and other unique earthly treasures. The fact is, she was often subject to toothaches.

She once received the French ambassador early one morning after a bad night of pain. He recorded that the queen was still in her morning nightgown when she received him, and wearing:

> ...a dress of silver cloth...the lining adorned with little pendants of rubies and pearls. On her head a garland of the same material and beneath it a great, reddish-colored wig with a great number of spangles of gold and silver and hanging down on her forehead some pearls.... Her face appears very aged. It is long and thin and her teeth are very yellow and unequal...and on the left side less than on her right. Many of them are missing so that one cannot understand her easily when she speaks quickly...

Poor Elizabeth! Although she is said to have eaten moderately at mealtimes and rarely to have drunk wine, preferring beer and ale, the sweets presented to her and eaten in happy quantities, were fatal for her teeth. Suckets, a type of candy, were very popular and were made of a variety of things. For example, lettuce, orange pips and green walnuts were dipped into boiling syrup, cooled and then re-dipped until they were thickly coated with hard sugar.

If she had a toothache, the queen was in bad humour, and when she was in bad humour, affairs of state suffered. On one such occasion, horribly swollen in the cheek from an infected tooth, the queen raged at anyone who dared approach her. Her personal doctor had tried what he could, but nothing availed. Councillors argued *ad infinitum* about what was to be done and, at length, agreed that they had nothing to lose by sending for a doctor by the name of John Fenatus. Dr. Fenatus was reputed to be able to cure all sorts of pain—and surely a toothache would be a simple matter for him.

Perhaps the toothache would have been a simple matter, if the queen had consented to open her mouth for Dr. Fenatus. She would not. Reciting various remedies in Latin, none of which were listened to by the English monarch, Dr. Fenatus eventually proposed extraction, which enraged the queen twice as much. She was terrified of surgery, and a glance at Dr. Fenatus' surgical instruments caused her royal heart to stand still.

"All right," said Dr. Fenatus to anyone who would listen, "fill the tooth with fenugreek and put some wax on top to hold it in place. In time, the tooth will loosen, and Her Majesty can remove it herself with her royal fingers. But," he added doggedly, "I am sure that pulling the tooth out right now would really benefit Her Majesty the most."

Elizabeth cowered. She withdrew to a corner in her room and one by one her councillors tried to persuade her to listen to Dr. Fenatus. Finally an old man, one Thomas Aylmer, the Bishop of London, came to speak with her.

"Your Majesty," he said, "I am an old man. I probably have less teeth left than years but would gladly give one to your Majesty."

She stared at him, holding her swollen cheek with a bejewelled hand, unable to speak.

"I will sit in yonder chair," went on Thomas Aylmer, "and have Dr. Fenatus draw out one of my teeth. Then your Majesty can see that the pain of having a tooth drawn is far less than you fear."

He then proceeded to do just that. He sat down in a chair and motioned that Dr. Fenatus approach with his surgical instruments. Before he opened his mouth for the extraction, he smiled at his queen. She remained in her corner but then, moved by both curiosity and his compassion, edged closer. Thomas Aylmer opened his mouth and bravely and unflinchingly endured the entirely unnecessary surgery.

Queen Elizabeth I was so encouraged by his example that she finally submitted to an extraction. And the affairs of state went on.

It is not to be concluded that everyone go out and do exactly likewise! But certainly Bishop Aylmer is to be commended for being faithful, for so sharing his sovereign's pain that he was willing to sacrifice a part of himself. And that is what sacrifice is all about, isn't it?

Food for thought

1. Why do you suppose Thomas Aylmer's approach to persuade Queen Elizabeth I to have her tooth extracted worked?

2. Why is sacrifice part of being a Christian?

09

Acts 9:1–6 *But Saul, still breathing threats and murder against the disciples of the Lord, went to the high priest and asked him for letters to the synagogues at Damascus, so that if he found any belonging to the Way, men or women, he might bring them bound to Jerusalem. Now as he went on his way, he approached Damascus, and suddenly a light from heaven flashed around him. And falling to the ground he heard a voice saying to him, "Saul, Saul, why are you persecuting me?" And he said, "Who are you, Lord?" And he said, "I am Jesus, whom you are persecuting. But rise and enter the city, and you will told what you are to do."*

Patrick's will

In the mid 1800s a young lad, a teenager, by the impressive name of Patrick William McConvill, was called in for a talk by his priest.

"Patrick, my lad," said the priest, looking fondly at the strapping boy, "you're a fine specimen of coming manhood, and the church could use more good boys like you."

Patrick grinned, more than a little relieved. He had thought the priest was going to give him a lecture on his behaviour as he'd been in more than one fight recently. Shrugging and shuffling his feet, he was still not totally comfortable, certain the priest had called him in for more than a compliment on his physique. And he was right.

"Patrick," the priest went on smoothly, "I'm sure it has not escaped your notice that here in Dundalk, here in this beautiful piece of Ireland, some people have tried to set up a heretic mission, which makes fools of our own Roman Catholic Church."

He paused for effect. Patrick stopped shuffling his feet and looked directly at him.

"Yes, father," he hesitantly responded.

"They visit houses," the priest's voice became louder, "and invite people to attend their evening meetings. And do you know what they tell them at these meetings, lad? They tell them not to go to Mass anymore."

"Not go to Mass?" Patrick repeated rather dully.

"Yes, my son," said the priest, moving his face closer to Patrick. "And we need young stalwart men, such as yourself and a few of your friends, to take down the names of those who are led astray by them, to teach them a lesson. Do you follow?"

Patrick nodded. He did, indeed, follow.

The Irish Church Mission to the Roman Catholics was a mission with a single purpose—to prayerfully teach that Jesus Christ had died for repentant sinners once and for all. House-to-house visits were carried out by dedicated missionaries in a number of cities in Ireland, and all those visited were invited to come to talks in which salvation in Christ was presented.

In the Dundalk neighbourhood, many people responded to these visits—too many for the priest's liking. Patrick William McConvill, however, at the priest's instigation, was only too happy to stand guard close to the mission entrance with a few of his tough friends. He challenged every single person who passed, and together with his rowdy crew, threw mud and stones at those who had the courage to step toward the mission's open door. Over the next few weeks, attendance dwindled. Most people were afraid to tangle with Patrick William McConvill's gang of thugs. Although they were interested in hearing the Bible explained, and although they appreciated the sincerity of the mission workers, they felt it was not worth getting beat up over.

One evening, the missionary who stood by the open door of the mission challenged William.

"My friend," he called out to the tall, gangly youth, "Paul says in the Bible, in 1 Timothy 2:5, there is but one God and one Mediator. But I will give you five pounds if you can show me a text that says there is one God and two mediators."

William shrugged. He had a smattering of Bible knowledge and he served at mass.

"There is no such text in the Douay Testament," he replied.

The missionary repeated his challenge a few times, but it was difficult over the yelling and cat-calls of the crowd to know whether the boy understood him. Great was his amazement, therefore, when Patrick William McConvill called on him the next morning to ask whether the text he had quoted was really and truly in the Douay Testament.

"Here is a Douay Testament," the missionary replied, "why don't you borrow it for a week and read for yourself?"

Within three days, Patrick was back. He had read the Scriptures, the Holy Spirit had blessed the reading and a light had gone on in his heart.

"You have spoken the truth," the boy said to the missionary, "and I understand enough to know I need never pray to either the Virgin Mary or the saints again."

He secretly visited the mission many times and came to firmly believe in Jesus as his only Lord and Saviour.

The story doesn't end here. William Patrick McConvill now went back to his parish church and freely spoke of his Saviour to other churchgoers, as well as to the priest. His conversion was not taken kindly. He was surrounded one day by the same sort of mob he himself used to lead, and was roughly tied up hand and foot and placed in a cart. Then, amid punches, jeers and taunts, he was driven to a neighbouring town where he was held captive. The mission notified the police and William was rescued. But even though he was rescued, it became nearly impossible for him to continue to live in Dundalk because of the hatred many people now had for him. He enlisted in the army and died some twenty-three years later, having witnessed to many of Jesus Christ, the only Mediator between God and man.

His will read, in part,

In the name of the Father, Son, and Holy Ghost. Amen. I, Patrick William McConvill, being of sound mind, hereby leave, by this deed of trust, the proceeds of my little effects to the Irish Church Mission to Roman Catholics, having first paid my debts as hereinafter named...I die in the faith of the Lord Jesus Christ, my only Saviour, in whom I am safe for ever...God is my Father, Christ is my Elder Brother, and only Priest, and I am comforted by the Holy Ghost. I know that to be absent from the body is to be present with the Lord.... May God send the gospel to all my fellow-countrymen in dear old Ireland.

Food for thought

1. Did William have to tell fellow churchgoers about his newly found faith? Why or why not? Can you prove your answer from the Bible?

2. What do you think Patrick left in his will and to whom did he leave it?

10

Isaiah 44:24–26 *Thus says the Lord, your Redeemer, who formed you in the womb: I am the Lord, who made all things, who alone stretched out the heavens, who spread out the earth by myself, who frustrates the signs of liars and makes fools of diviners, who turns wise men back and makes their knowledge foolish, who confirms the word of his servant and fulfills the counsel of his messengers.*

Bickerstaff stuff

Almost 300 years ago, a fellow by the name of Isaac Bickerstaff published a paper which he distributed freely. Unfortunately, no one had ever heard of Isaac Bickerstaff before. But as it is with people, when they read something interesting, they often don't care who has written it. If their sense of interest has been piqued; if they learn something they perceive to be amazing, they generally don't bother to research sources. The unknown Isaac Bickerstaff claimed to be an astrologer. The paper he published and distributed freely was an almanac. In it, he predicted the death by fever of another astrologer of that day, a John Partridge. He said that Mr. Partridge would die on March 29 of that year, which was, by the way, 1708. People were intrigued. Mr. Partridge was well-known. His astrology predictions were widely read. Many believed that Mr. Bickerstaff must surely be very knowledgeable in order to foretell the future so precisely.

Mr. Partridge, upon reading Mr. Bickerstaff's pamphlet, was understandably upset. He had no desire to die and resented someone else saying he was to die imminently. His own astrological predictions were lucrative, and he loved the land of the living. Mr. Partridge therefore indignantly denied Bickerstaff's prophecy about his demise. Mr. Bickerstaff, however, not put off in the least, printed another pamphlet that he distributed on March 30, the day after the predicted death. In it, he said that his prediction had come true and Mr. Partridge had indeed died. People read the announcement avidly and talked about it in the streets and taverns.

"Partridge has really died. Did you know?"

On April 1, John Partridge was woken by a sexton outside his window.

"Do you have," the man asked, in all seriousness, "any orders for your funeral sermon?"

Irritated, John closed the shutters, got dressed and went for a walk. But, no matter where he went that day, people stared at him as if he were a ghost. There were even some who stopped him to tell him that he looked exactly like John Partridge. Hard as he tried, he was unable to convince people he was not dead.

Bickerstaff was actually none other than the author Jonathan Swift (1667–1745). His articles on Partridge were swallowed hook, line and sinker by the public of his day. John Partridge, as a result of these articles, had to stop making astrological predictions because people did not believe him anymore. Perhaps, this is what Swift had in mind in the first place. After all, it is said in Isaiah that God will frustrate the signs of liars and make fools of diviners (Isaiah 44:25).

Faith in something or someone is an intangible thing. A lot of people who actually saw and touched Partridge refused to believe he was alive. Such unbelief was, and is, nothing new. Think of all those who refuse to believe in Jesus, who truly died and is alive.

Bickerstaff stuff has always happened. One of the silliest stories of this last century took place in 1957. The BBC announced in the spring of that year that, due to a relatively mild winter and because of the eradication of the lethal spaghetti weevil, Swiss farmers were enjoying a bumper spaghetti crop. They had live footage of Swiss peasants pulling strands of spaghetti down from trees. The amazing thing is that hundreds of viewers called the television station wanting to know where they could get spaghetti trees. They were told, by those who answered the phone, they should place a sprig of spaghetti in a tin of tomato sauce and hope for the best.

The very same type of people who would cheerfully pick spaghetti off trees, do not believe Jonah was swallowed by a fish or that Jesus was born of a virgin. They mock the resurrection and find fault with a literal Bible.

Many strange claims have been made in the past and are still being made today. The challenge is to sort out the foolish from the true.

The apostle Paul claimed to be a fool for Christ's sake. His devotion to God's truth was such that people thought him foolish. So there is in fact a true foolishness.

Food for thought

1. Proverbs 26:18–19 says: "Like a madman who throws firebrands, arrows, and death, is the man who deceives his neighbor and says, 'I am only joking!'" Have you ever played an April Fool's joke on someone? What is the difference between a harmless joke and a lie? Or, is there no difference?

2. Are there any truths in the Bible that you find difficult to believe? What are they? What is faith? (Check out Hebrews 11:1.)

11

Deuteronomy 30:19–20 *I call heaven and earth to witness against you today, that I have set before you life and death, blessing and curse. Therefore choose life, that you and your offspring may live, loving the Lord your God, obeying his voice, and holding fast to him, for he is your life and length of days.*

The ugly duckling
PART 1

O nce upon a time, there lived in the town of Odense, on the island of Fyn in Denmark, a poor shoemaker. Although this opening line almost sounds like the beginning of a fairy tale, this is a true story, and it begins in the early 1800s.

The poor shoemaker, whose name was Hans, fell in love with a poor washerwoman. Her name was Ane-Marie. They married and set up house, but were so poor that they had to make most of their furniture themselves. The bed they slept in was originally a wooden frame that had been used to hold the coffin of a count. Pieces of black cloth still stuck to it. In 1805, however, the somber bed was filled with the joyful sound of a newborn's wail. Ane-Marie gave birth to a boy—a blond, thin, long, little boy—a baby who was christened Hans Christian Anderson.

Hans Christian's father, the shoemaker, was a dreamer. When he was not making shoes, he read to his son and made him toys and a puppet theatre. There was only one tiny room in the house, and it was filled to capacity with a shoemaker's bench, the bed and Hans Christian's trundle crib. Each day, Ane-Marie cleaned the room before she went to the river to wash other people's laundry, and each day Hans worked at his shoemaker's bench while Hans Christian played with his toys, made up stories and sang songs.

Father Hans was not a very good shoemaker and never made much money. There was little to eat and clothes were shabby and threadbare. Not only that, but Hans Christian, thin and long-legged like a stork, grew so fast that his clothes were usually ill-fitting as well. And his shoes were made of wood.

Schools at that time cost money and attendance was not compulsory. A poor child usually became apprenticed to a carpenter or a tailor, never seeing the inside of a schoolroom. But father Hans wanted his son to have a better life than he did so he sent Hans Christian to school. Hans Christian didn't care for school routine, however, nor the fact that the other children laughed at him. They made him feel poor and ugly. He ran home and refused to return. And no one made him return.

At night as he lay in his small trundle bed, Hans Christian listened drowsily to his father reading aloud to his mother by the light of a single candle. Sometimes his father read the Bible, and one night Hans Christian heard him say, "Christ *was* only a man like us, but he was an extraordinary man." His mother was appalled and called this blasphemy. Hans Christian shivered in bed and expected the roof to fall, but nothing happened. However, his father's words stayed with him. A father's words often stay with a child his whole life. That is why it is such a great responsibility to be a father. As it was, Hans Christian developed a childlike faith, not in God, but in the innate goodness of life and of humankind.

Hans Christian was eight when his father died. A poor man with a thin face—and an even thinner hope for eternity. The child and his mother were quite alone. When Hans Christian was thirteen, his mother remarried. It was another poor shoemaker and one who paid little attention to his stepson. It was time to go and seek his proverbial fortune. And Hans Christian did.

Food for thought

1. Does what your father believes have a great impact on your life? How so?

2. When fathers and mothers do not teach their children the truth of the gospel message of Jesus Christ, they are, in a sense, sacrificing their children to the world. Comment on this statement.

12

Isaiah 17:10–11 *For you have forgotten the God of your salvation and have not remembered the Rock of your refuge; therefore, though you plant pleasant plants and sow the vine-branch of a stranger, though you make them grow on the day that you plant them, and make them blossom in the morning that you sow, yet the harvest will flee away in a day of grief and incurable pain.*

The ugly duckling
PART 2

Leaving a weeping mother and grandmother behind, a ferry took Hans Christian to the mainland. All he owned was a small bundle of clothes, his puppet theatre and some bread. But he felt quite sure that fame was waiting for him in Copenhagen. Dressed like a scarecrow in an old suit that had belonged to his father, and sporting a hat that fell over his eyes, he arrived in the capital of Denmark. Determined to be an actor, he doggedly knocked on doors, begged for audiences, prayed for God's help and somehow survived several years.

When Hans Christian was seventeen years old, he submitted a

play to the directors of the Copenhagen Theatre. Full of grammatical and spelling errors, it merited little praise. Somehow, through all the hodgepodge of words and ideas, the directors sensed a small glimmer of talent. Denmark had a fund for artists and writers and promising people were given money for living expenses and tuition. The King of Denmark, on the recommendation of the directors, approved Hans Christian's name for this fund. So, at the age of seventeen, Hans Christian was put in the second grade at a grammar school about fifty miles from Copenhagen.

The four ensuing years were something of a nightmare for the boy. Tall and lanky to begin with, Hans Christian towered over his much younger classmates. The rector of the school disliked him, and made fun of him at every opportunity. Grammar, geography and mathematics were all new to him. Hans Christian worked as hard as he could. He was petrified of the rector, who continued to call him names and belittle him in front of all the other students. Fortunately, after four-and-a-half years of this, a friend reported the cruelty to the Board of Directors. They promptly took him away from the school and found a private tutor, a Mr. Muller, to help Hans Christian continue his studies.

Mr. Muller was a fine tutor and one who held the Bible as infallible. He helped Hans Christian prepare for his university examination, giving him encouragement and friendship. Hans Christian argued with him about religion and about Jesus being a good man and not God. Mr. Muller plainly warned Hans Christian that he was in danger of hellfire if he did not accept Jesus as the One who saves from sins. Hans Christian remained content in the belief that God was love and that he rewarded people for living a good life.

Hans Christian passed his university examination very well and his Copenhagen sponsors were proud of him. Given a small pension by the king, he was full of confidence. He rented a room and began writing in earnest—poems, plays, opera stories and travel books. Gentle and very emotional, Hans Christian loved to hear praise from others about his work. On the other hand, if someone criticized him, he was apt to burst into tears.

In 1834, Hans Christian wrote a book called *The Improvisator*. It was really the story of his own life. He was sure the book would be a success. Being a little short of money, at this time, he also penned some small stories, tales he called them, and brought them to a publisher. The first story was called *The Tinder Box*, the second *Little Claus and Big Claus* and the third *The Princess and the Pea*. These stories were published in 1835 when Hans Christian was thirty years old.

The little book of tales sold so well, that the publisher encouraged Hans Christian to write more. He did, and they were very popular. All over the world, his tales were translated and read; all over the world, children and adults alike read stories by the son of the poor shoemaker and the poor washerwoman. Denmark, his home country, was the last to realize how wonderful an author he really was.

Hans Christian wanted very much to marry and have a loving home, but he felt he was too ugly for anyone to love him. When he wrote *The Little Mermaid*, a story many people have read, he poured all his sadness of being alone into it. The little mermaid was never able to reach her heart's desire of winning the prince for her husband. But she was so good and kind that she received another reward in the story. It was Hans Christian's philosophy of life—God is good and he rewards those who are good.

Hans Christian's sense of God was simple and child-like. But it was not the triune God he worshipped, for he still believed, as his father had instilled in him, that Jesus was a only a good man—a man whose love and simplicity in living were an example to all.

There were times, in his old age, that Hans Christian dined with the King of Denmark. His life situation was now a far cry from the poor shoemaker's one-room house. Grey-haired, he was still thin and tall with huge hands and feet, but he had become a beloved storyteller to many people.

In 1875, Hans Christian Anderson died. It is reported that he died peacefully in his sleep. Few people, when they visit Denmark, go to visit his grave. Instead they flock to see the reading statue made of him, or they stare for a long time at the statue of the Little Mermaid at Langelinie. In this way, they remember Hans Christian. But the question is not whether people will remember Hans Christian—the question is, will God remember him?

Food for thought

1. Hans was given the opportunity to see truth in that he was given an older man, a tutor, to warn him that he was on the wrong path. How has God been patient with you?

2. Why is it more important that God remembers you than that anyone else remembers you? Explain.

13

Romans 5:6-9 *For while we were still weak, at the right time Christ died for the ungodly. For one will scarcely die for a righteous person—though perhaps for a good person one would dare even to die—but God shows his love for us in that while we were still sinners, Christ died for us. Since, therefore, we have now been justified by his blood, much more shall we be saved by him from the wrath of God.*

Justified by his blood

There are many stories about the Covenanters of Scotland—those courageous men and women who stood up for religious freedom in that country during the 1600s. Some of the stories are true and others are the stuff legends are made of. There is one such story, perhaps it is a legend, which teaches much about the quality of compassion. As a matter of fact, it faintly mirrors the great love God has for his people in Christ Jesus.

There was a Scottish woman who, aware that there was a large contingent of pillaging soldiers behind her who had massacred most of the people in her village, ran as fast as she could across a meadow one evening at dusk. A dog ran at her side, and she carried a child. Had she set the boy down and left him, she might have been quicker and escaped without the soldiers' knowledge. But she loved the child and could not do it. She held the lad in her arms and ran. Breathing heavily, she thought she could not take another step when she at last reached the road. There was a river next to the road. And spanning the river—a bridge. The woman half stumbled, half fell down the embankment, and just before the soldiers behind her were visible, crept underneath its protecting shelter.

Holding her hand over the child's mouth, she shivered in anticipation. The dog, who had not left her side since she first began her exodus, sat by her side. Soon the woman heard the soldiers advancing. The child, not understanding what was happening, struggled in her arms. She held him tighter and rocked back and forth. The boy, eyes wide open, looked at his mother. The water sloshed gently against the shore, and the soldiers passed over the bridge. She heard them and held her breath. They crossed noisily. Boots stomping. Muskets rattling. Men whistling. She waited silently, pressing against the stone wall, willing the men above her to move on and out of sight. The dog, tongue hanging out of his mouth, didn't move an inch. She almost dared not breathe. And the soldiers kept on passing, until the sound of their company faded—faded even as the sun was fading fast.

It became quiet and still, yet she dared not move. But at length, having stood some ten minutes after the last footfall had passed overhead, she took her hand away from the boy's mouth and smiled down at him. He smiled back, even laughed in delight. And then to her horror, she heard a voice above her, on the bridge.

"What was that noise, Jack?"

The reply came softly.

"I don't know, sir."

"Well, I can tell you what it was. It was a child—a child hiding under this bridge, Jack. Go down and make an end of him."

The next instant a man came sliding down the embankment, a young man, not yet twenty years old. He saw the mother instantly and their eyes locked. She was ready to die, he noted—but the child, she could not stomach the child dying. She held it in her arms, her left hand over his mouth to keep him from making more noise. The boy's blue eyes looked at the soldier wonderingly and the dog's hackles stood straight up as it bared its teeth. At a motion from the woman, the animal lay down. The fellow made a split second decision. He strode forward, bayonet gleaming in the darkened area, and drove the sharp end deep into the dog. The animal rolled over with a small whimper. The bayonet dripped red. The woman did not move as the soldier turned and climbed back up the embankment to the bridge.

"That's a lot of blood," the officer said, and then went on, "and I don't believe it's human blood. That was a dog's whimper I heard just now. Must I go down and do the job myself? Go back and kill the child or I will kill you."

The soldier turned and slid down the embankment once more. The woman stood exactly where he had left her. The dog lay at her feet and the river ran on as calmly as if nothing had happened. The soldier drew his sabre, and in one quick motion grabbed the child's hand, cutting off one of the boy's fingers. The child screamed. But the scream was halted by the mother, who stuffed her plaid into his mouth as she silently watched the soldier smear the blood onto his sword. A second later, he was gone. After a minute or so, she heard both men leave, and she was finally left alone—alone with a dead dog and a bleeding child.

Many, many years later, a soldier, travelling through that same region, was in need of overnight shelter. He stopped and asked for the hospitality of one of the cottages he passed. The owner of the small home invited him in, gave him supper and allowed him a place by the fire.

"I see you're a soldier," said the peasant as his wife and children stared at the visitor's bayonet.

The man nodded his assent.

"And what," the peasant went on, "was the worst thing you have ever seen in all your years of soldiering?"

The man hesitated somewhat before answering.

"It was a long time ago," he then said, speaking slowly, "and it was a battle that took place not too far from here—a battle at Glencoe."

The peasant drew in his breath sharply.

"You were at that battle?"

"Yes," the soldier answered wearily, as he looked into the flames, "and it was truly the most terrible thing I have ever..."

He stopped and sighed. The peasant did not press the matter but offered to bring the man to his bed in the loft. After having brought him to the room over the stable, he came back inside.

"I will make an end of him in the morning," he said to his wife, "for were not our grandparents killed at Glencoe, and shouldn't I avenge their blood?"

His wife shook her head.

"You must ask him more about the battle," she answered, "What if you are mistaken?"

The next morning, at breakfast, the soldier was again asked what he knew of Glencoe. The man told his host the story of a little child, hidden under a bridge with his mother and a dog. The peasant abruptly pushed back his chair and walked to the door. He opened it and stood in the doorway, looking outside for a long time. Then he turned and held up his right hand—a hand from which the little finger was missing. The soldier and the peasant parted as friends.

The soldier was saved from death and was put into a right relationship with the peasant because of the blood of a little finger. Even so, sinners are put into a right relationship with God through, not a sinful little finger, but the innocent blood of Jesus Christ, his Son.

Food for thought

1. Recall a time that you were so angry with someone, you thought you might kill him or her. Why do you think God might be justified in sentencing you to death?

2. Discuss the following phrase: "Believers need not become alarmed about any divine wrath, now or in the future."

14

Proverbs 28:13 *Whoever conceals his transgressions will not prosper, but he who confesses and forsakes them will obtain mercy.*

Find mercy

In a story that takes place in Ayr, Scotland, during the 1800s, the effects of not telling the truth come across rather vividly.

It seems that a man by the name of Bailie Saunders, a tanner and a member of the town council, was a respected elder in the church's Session (or consistory). Bailie was well liked, wealthy and often led the church service when the minister was not in town.

It happened one day that Bailie had to travel to Glasgow on business. He went there by coach, arrived safely, concluded his business that afternoon, had tea and went for a walk—all in that order. As he was enjoying the beautiful weather, he noticed that a large crowd had gathered in front of the theatre down the street. Now theatre was anathema to staunch Reformed Presbyterians, and Bailie walked on, fully intending to pass the group. He approached the edge of the crowd and was stopped by its very size blocking the sidewalk. He stood for a minute, uncertain as to what to do and how to get past. But, at that moment, people queued up beside him and behind him, so that he was literally hemmed in. As he tried to jostle his way through, the theatre doors were opened and the surging movement of people carried him straight to the ticket office. For a brief second, his conscience smote him, but then, impelled on a whim, he bought a ticket and entered with the others.

Bailie got a good seat, and was very much entertained by the play. As a matter of fact, he was so entertained that when it was over he clapped and cheered enthusiastically, standing on his seat while throwing his hat into the air. The next day, rather ashamed of his worldly conduct, he travelled back home, glad that no one had seen him.

But, as these things go, Bailie's misstep was not to remain hidden. About two weeks after the incident, rumours began to fly in Ayr that one of their local citizens had been seen in a theatre in Glasgow. Horrors! And such was the power of the gossip, that the name of the culprit (which was said to be not Bailie but a man named Williams) was given. The elders were informed, and a meeting of Session was called.

The minister who led the Session did not for a moment believe that Mr. Williams was guilty. He said that Williams had been an upright, generous and faithful church member for years and years and said that it was beneath the Session's dignity to indulge these horrendous rumours. Every one of the Session members agreed with him. They all felt that there was just no possibility that Mr. Williams might be guilty of the gossipers' accusation. But, because there was the matter of the reality of the slander, they did think Mr. Williams should be approached. He need only say "I haven't been to the theatre," they concurred, and the whole matter would be dropped. And, in spite of his protestations, Bailie Saunders was the Session member assigned to visit Mr. Williams.

For the next few days, Bailie Saunders dawdled. He did this

and that and just could not bring himself to visit Mr. Williams. Finally, there was no putting it off, and with an uneasy conscience, he put on his coat, and set a course for Williams' office. Heartily welcomed, he was asked to come in, and offered a comfortable chair. He began with an apology.

"There's a bad rumour going around," he said, "and, no doubt, you'll soon deny it, concerning your character."

"What" said Mr. Williams, turning pale, "is the rumour?"

Bailie took a drink from the glass of spirits Mr. Williams had given him when he first sat down, and then he got to the point.

"That you have attended the theatre in Glasgow!" he threw out.

Mr. Williams was silent for a bit. Then he replied in a low voice.

"I went to Glasgow a while ago. That is true. While I was walking down a street, I noticed a huge crowd in front of a theatre. In the crowd I saw an old friend."

Here he stopped, and Bailie felt himself growing cold. He swallowed audibly.

"The old friend," continued Mr. Williams, "went in and I followed him, but to do so I had to buy a ticket for the gallery. Forced to spend the evening there, in such a wicked place, I resolved never to return."

Bailie wrung his hands.

"Oh, Mr. Williams. Were you not afraid to go into such a place?"

Mr. Williams stared at him a while before he resumed his tale.

"My friend—the man whom I told you I followed—sat in the centre of the theatre. After the performance, he stood up in his chair and cheered. There was no mistaking you Bailie Saunders."

Bailie looked down, more ashamed then he had yet felt up to this point and then told Mr. Williams he need not worry, that he would take care of telling the Session.

When Session next met, Bailie simply informed them that Mr. Williams had not been to the theatre and that this was the truth. All rejoiced and shook hands. The minister prayed a prayer of thankfulness that no sin had been committed.

That night, however, Bailie could not sleep. His conscience smote him heavier than before, so that sweat broke out from every pore in his body. In the morning, he hurried over to Mr. Williams' office and confessed how he had deceived his fellow elders. As he was talking, the minister came in to congratulate Mr. Williams on having unscathingly passed under gossip.

Both Mr. Williams and Bailie Saunders sat quietly under the minister's good wishes. Then Bailie arose, whispered something in Mr. Williams' ear, after which he related the whole matter to the pastor. Then both men wrote out a confession—a confession which was read to the Session and from the pulpit of the congregation. The next Sunday, thoroughly humbled, both Mr. Williams and Bailie Saunders stood up, each in his church pew, and accepted a stern rebuke from the minister after the service.

It is said that many in the congregation cried, but it is also said that many rejoiced because sinners had turned from their way back into the fold.

Food for thought

1. Do you think we should have public confessions in church today, whether it be from attending x-rated movies, reading ungodly books, speaking gossip, having unethical business dealings, etc.? Why or why not?

2. What does this proverb mean: "Whoever conceals his transgressions will not prosper, but he who confesses and forsakes them will obtain mercy" (Proverbs 28:13)?

15

1 Peter 3:1–2 *Likewise, wives, be subject to your own husbands, so that even if some do not obey the word, they may be won without a word by the conduct of their wives, when they see your respectful and pure conduct.*

Clothilde's conduct

Clothilde was a princess. Her father's name was Chilperic, King of Burgundy. Born in A.D. 475, she was raised as a Christian. Burgundy was a small kingdom in what is now southern France, on the border of Italy. A devout girl, imagine Clothilde's shock when her father told her that he had betrothed her to Clovis, King of the Franks. On the one hand, she knew that Clovis, who was twenty-seven, nine years older than her own eighteen years, was a fearless young man. At the tender age of fifteen, he had succeeded his father, Childeric. And seven years later, when he was twenty-two, he had courageously taken up arms against the last Roman governor of Gaul, Syagrius, and had beaten him thoroughly. Even her own ladies-in-waiting praised him for this action. On the other hand, she knew Clovis was a pagan who worshipped gods of wood and stone.

Whether or not Clothilde protested to her father that she could not marry a pagan, is not known. The truth of the matter is that she married Clovis, and by doing so became the queen of the Frankish people.

In the course of time, Clothilde bore Clovis a child. Clovis was pleased. He found his little Burgundian queen obedient and loving, and she brought him joy. The baby was a boy, and he had wanted a son—a son to carry on the Merovingian dynasty he had started. (Merewig was the name of Clovis' grandfather.) But he was not so smitten with his new wife that he would give in to the request she made of him.

"Please let me have the baby baptized."

"No," he answered plainly and simply, "I do not believe in your God and will not let my child partake in a ceremony in which your God is acknowledged."

Clothilde pleaded with Clovis, using logic.

"The gods you worship," she said, "are not real. They're carved out of wood and stone. Their names are mortal and their stories silly."

It didn't matter that Clovis shushed her, that he walked away or that he lost his temper with her. Clothilde was adamant that their child should be baptized into the name of the one true God, and at every opportunity she would speak of him.

In the end, Clovis gave in, and there was a baptism. The baby was named Ingomer. But after the baptism, while still wearing the ornate, baptismal robes, the infant became ill and died in Clothilde's arms. Clovis was livid with sorrow and rage, and he reproached Clothilde for the child's death.

"If the baby had been dedicated in the name of my gods," he yelled, "there is no question that he would have lived. But because he was baptized in the name of your God he died."

There was a second child—another son. Strangely enough, in spite of what he believed had happened to his first son, Clovis permitted this second child to be baptized as well. This boy was named Chlodomer. Chlodomer, even as his brother, sickened after the church ceremony.

"What do you expect," Clovis contemptuously spewed out the words as he watched Clothilde rock the sick child. "He will also die as our first child died. No sooner are they baptized into the name of your Christ and they die."

Clothilde put the baby in the cradle. Then she knelt at its side and prayed earnestly. God was pleased to hear her prayer. Chlodomer recovered. But Clovis had no change of heart.

Then in the year A.D. 496, when little Chlodomer was a toddler, war broke out against the fierce tribe of the Alemanni. As Clovis stood on the battlefield at the head of his troops, he felt a chilling premonition of death. As they stormed toward the Alemanni, it became apparent before too long that Clovis' men were being slaughtered mercilessly. Clovis looked up at the sky, and moved within his heart by something he did not understand, he called out to his wife's God.

> Jesus Christ, you who Clothilde maintains to be the Son of the living God. You who deign to give help to those in travail and victory to those who trust in you, in faith I beg the glory of your help. If you will give me victory over my enemies, and if I may have evidence of that miracle power which the people dedicated to your name say they have experienced, then I will believe in you, and I will be baptized in your name. I have called upon my own gods but, as I see only too clearly, they have no intention of helping me. I therefore cannot believe that they possess any power, for they do not come to the assistance of those who trust them. I now call upon you. I want to believe in you, but I must first be saved from my enemies.

Even as Clovis spoke, a contingent of the Alemanni suddenly turned and began to run. Their king had been killed, and deflated by the loss of their leader, they lost heart. The troops that were left behind submitted to Clovis.

Later, back home, with a certain amount of incredulity, Clovis told Clothilde what had happened. Clothilde put it to him that he was now without excuse: he was now obliged to accept God as his

Lord. Clovis made no protest, nor did he refuse Christian instruction. As well, he spoke to his warriors with the result that they also consented to be baptized.

Food for thought

1. What do you think of Clothilde's conduct throughout the story? Was it in keeping with what God requires of a godly wife? Why or why not?

2. In the years following his baptism, Clovis often did things that were not good. Do you think that Clovis' "conversion" to Christianity was a matter of the heart? Is it important that we know this? Why or why not?

16

Hebrews 9:11–14 *But when Christ appeared as a high priest of the good things that have come, then through the greater and more perfect tent (not made with hands, that is, not of this creation) he entered once for all into the holy places, not by means of the blood of goats and calves but by means of his own blood, thus securing an eternal redemption. For if the blood of goats and bulls, and the sprinkling of defiled persons with the ashes of a heifer, sanctify for the purification of the flesh, how much more will the blood of Christ, who through the eternal Spirit offered himself without blemish to God, purify our conscience from dead works to serve the living God.*

Conscience stricken

A Belgian once visited Scotland. While there, he toured a Scottish burial place—an old, old cemetery. Impressed by the ancient site, he coveted a stone for a souvenir. Surreptitiously he picked up a rock from between the monuments. It weighed a little over two pounds, so it was small enough to be hidden within the folds of his jacket. And, when you come to think of it, what's a stone? No one would miss it—certainly not the long-dead bodies beneath the earth.

Nevertheless, when the Belgian returned home, a series of mishaps caused him to stop and think. His daughter broke her leg; he lost his job; and his wife became ill. He began to reflect that perhaps these bad (or sad) events had to do with the fact that he had taken the rock. The pocketed stone consequently began to weigh heavier and heavier within the lining of his jacket. Had taking the stone perhaps been more important than he thought? After all, the burial site, Clava Cairs, was an ancient site, dating back to roughly 2000 B.C., and it was considered one of the most important and most mysterious locations in Scotland. Although he told himself repeatedly that the rock in his pocket was simply one of many similar rocks, and although he was convinced that in the long run it shouldn't make one bit of difference whether this particular rock was in Belgium or in Scotland, he could not get rid of the uncomfortable feeling that he had done something wrong.

The upshot of the matter was that the man sent the rock back to Scotland. He packed it up and sent it to the tourist office in Inverness along with an anonymous letter. In the letter he apologized for taking the rock and asked them to please return the rock to its rightful place in the cemetery. His letter was a trifle strange but he did not care. He firmly believed that his bad luck was being caused by the theft, and the deed was haunting him.

This anecdote is not the first time a theft, or a wrongdoing has caused a person to feel uncomfortable and return something that did not belong to him. As a matter of fact, there is an English term for such situations. The term is "conscience money." This is money paid anonymously to the British government by people who have cheated the government and who have, humanly speaking, gotten away with it. Their conscience becoming uneasy, they are able to anonymously send the deficit to the treasury department. This sum is then advertised in the newspaper so that they can see it has been received.

A conscience is not the peculiar possession of a Christian. All human beings have a conscience. God has equipped each person with a sense of right and wrong—whether that person is a believer or not. The etymology, or root, of the word conscience is *knowledge along with* (or shared with) a person. It is a person's inner sense of right and wrong. God has written this on a person's heart (Romans 2:14–15).

The Belgian tourist was reading God's law in his heart. He was listening to the voice of his God-given conscience, even though he did not realize it and even though he felt that he was being haunted.

Sometimes God causes conscience to produce a tremendous, immediate turn-about in a life. Richard Wurmbrand, in his book *In the Face of Surrender*, records a story about conscience and renewal.

In Sofia, Bulgaria, a Christian, imprisoned by the Communists, was put into a cell the size of a man. There were nails on the cell walls that pressed into his flesh at the slightest movement. When the door was locked, the prisoner's first words were: "Father, forgive them, for they know not what they do." When the warden asked the prisoner what these words meant, he was given the joyful account of the Gospel. As a result, the warden's conscience was smitten, and he opened the door. Later, when the arresting officer came, he found both the prisoner and the warden kneeling in prayer. The warden calmly told the officer that he was no longer under his orders but that he belonged to Jesus Christ. As a result, he too was imprisoned.

These two stories provide an interesting comparison. For the Belgian, his conscience was pricked so that he eventually returned the stolen rock. For the prison warden, his conscience was pricked *and* his heart was opened to the power of Christ's cleansing blood. We don't need just the power of a sensitive conscience but the saving work of Christ to make us new.

Food for thought

1. Is being conscience-stricken a sign that you are saved? Why or why not?

2. When you feel guilty about something, what do you do about it and why?

17

Psalm 8 *O Lord, our Lord, how majestic is your name in all the earth! You have set your glory above the heavens. Out of the mouth of babes and infants, you have established strength because of your foes, to still the enemy and the avenger. When I look at your heavens, the work of your fingers, the moon and the stars, which you have set in place, what is man that you are mindful of him, and the son of man that you care for him? Yet you have made him a little lower than the heavenly beings and crowned him with glory and honor. You have given him dominion over the works of your hands; you have put all things under his feet, all sheep and oxen, and also the beasts of the field, the birds of the heavens, and the fish of the sea, whatever passes along the paths of the seas. O Lord, our Lord, how majestic is your name in all the earth!*

Crowns

The use of a crown dates back to ancient times. It is a symbol of both victory and of martyrdom; it is associated with peace as well as war; it has been finely wrought with laurels, gold or jewels. Men have killed for it and worn it both honourably and dishonourably.

There are a number of "crown" stories of kings and queens— stories hidden away in the past, tucked behind the corners of time —stories from which we can glean a bit of understanding if we are discerning. One such story speaks of Gustavus Vasa, King of the Swedes. After an eventful life and reign this king retired in 1560.

On the day he was to leave the public eye, he made his way into the huge Hall of Assembly where his three sons, all his senators and many of his subjects were gathered. In this place, King Gustavus had his last will and testament read, after which he resigned his office.

> I have passed through many dangers during my forty years of reign, but by these grey locks, and the furrows time has planted in this countenance, I swear to you that the love of my people has been the end and arm of all my actions. If I have done aught acceptable in my government, be the glory to God; for such faults as my human weakness may have fallen into, they are mine alone. But you, my beloved subjects, will forgive me for them. My weakened body gives me many a proof that I am now speaking to you for the last time, and must shortly appear before the King of all kings, to give an account of my stewardship. Follow me with your prayers; do not forget me in your assemblies, and when my eyes are closed in death, leave my dust uncensored and undisturbed to its repose.

After saying this, Gustavus stretched out his hands and blessed all the people. Everyone was in tears. He then left, leaning on his two elder sons, but often looking back over his shoulders, saying farewell to all he passed. This was Gustavus' last public act. Three months later, he died. Gustavus acknowledged God as supreme and, although a crowned king, died a subject.

Frederick II, also known as The Magnificent or Holy Roman Emperor (1194–1250), was a king of an altogether different feather. A man versed in geometry, astrology and history, he could speak several languages and was a patron of the arts and sciences as well as a poet and scientist in his own right. But although learned, he had not the strength of faith in God that Gustavus had. Indeed, his faith seemed to be rooted in himself and his own accomplishments. During the course of his life, Frederick had acquired seven trophies—seven crowns. These crowns made up his empire and consisted of Germany, Lombardy, Burgundy, Sicily, Sardinia, Jerusalem and the rest of the Roman Empire. Shortly before his death, as he lay on his bed, he called for a servant to place these crowns before him on a table. There they glistened even as the last sweat glistened on his forehead. There lay the iron crown of Lombardy, covered with emeralds and said to have been made of the nails used at the crucifixion; there stood Charlemagne's crown with its jewels and inscriptions; and there glittered all the other diadems besides. With the death rattle in his throat, Frederick, eagerly eyeing the crowns, exclaimed hoarsely so that all around his bed could hear.

"I still possess them all and no pope shall deprive me of one of them."

Foolish man! Holding on to all, he held nothing.

Think for a moment on poet James Shirley's well-known verse. He lived a long time ago (1596–1666), but he had the right idea.

> The glories of our blood and state
>   Are shadows, not substantial things;
> There is no armor against fate;
> Death lays his icy hand on kings:
> Scepter and crown must tumble down,
>   And in the dust be equal made
>   With the poor crooked scythe and spade.

Shirley's thoughts are reflected in the actions of George III of England. After he was crowned, he partook of the Lord's Supper. Speaking softly to the Archbishop of Canterbury, he asked whether or not he should lay aside his crown for the celebration of this sacrament. The archbishop asked the Dean of Westminster but neither of them knew.

"There is no form or procedure to go by," the archbishop finally told the king.

The king thereupon took off his crown, saying, "There ought to be one."

Food for thought

1. Keeping in mind Psalm 8, it is clear that all men have been crowned by God. What exactly does that mean for you?

2. All Christians are in a race for the victor's crown (1 Corinthians 9:24–26). How should you run your race—live your life—so that you will obtain a victory wreath?

18

Revelation 6:9–11 *When he opened the fifth seal, I saw under the altar the souls of those who had been slain for the word of God and for the witness they had borne. They cried out with a loud voice, "O Sovereign Lord, holy and true, how long before you will judge and avenge our blood on those who dwell on the earth?" Then they were each given a white robe and told to rest a little longer, until the number of their fellow servants and their brothers should be complete, who were to be killed as they themselves had been.*

Foxe of Lincolnshire

John Foxe was born in Boston, Lincolnshire in 1517, the same year that Martin Luther posted his theses at Wittenberg. But baby John had no idea what the theses meant and slept through the initial Reformation furor quite contentedly.

John's father died when he was very young, and his mother remarried. The gentleman was Richard Melton. John seems to have been fond of Mr. Melton, and it seems that Mr. Melton was fond of the boy as well, because he gladly paid for his stepson's schooling. Perhaps this was because John was very little trouble. From the time that the child could distinguish his first letters, he was known as a devoted bookworm. When other boys went out to play, John would stay behind; and when search was made, he was usually found in church at prayers or curled up in some small nook reading to himself, lost to the world. An honest boy who, by the grace of God, developed good character traits, he was, in due time, sent off to Oxford.

In Oxford, through much Bible reading, John Foxe became a devout Protestant. He knew that by becoming one, he was joining his heart to a religion in which you had to be willing to make sacrifices. In 1538, while he was still at Oxford, a Protestant named William Cowbridge was burned at the stake. Foxe witnessed the burning, and it impressed him deeply.

After his conversion, some of John's Roman Catholic fellow students began to throw questions at him—questions such as "Why are you hardly ever at Chapel?" or "Why shun our society?" and "Why are you not taking part in recreation with us any more?" Gossip, finger-pointing and accusations made his life very miserable.

Although John Foxe was studying for the priesthood, his strong Protestant views on marriage put him in a predicament. It was obvious he could not be both priest and Protestant. At the end of his studies, John was offered a tutorship near Stratford. It was here he met and wed Agnes Randall, a godly woman.

The year 1547 found John Foxe out of work and broke. He spent much time in church on his knees. One day he was sitting in St. Paul's Cathedral, thin with fasting and worry, when a stranger sat down next to him. After greeting him in a friendly fashion, the man took Foxe's hand and pressed a sum of money into it.

"Be of good cheer," he said, "I know not what your troubles may be, but they seem from your appearance to be no light ones; so do not refuse from your countryman a gift which common kindness impels me to offer. Go home, recover your spirits, and begin to live again. Fresh hope is at hand: within a few days you will find a more certain means of livelihood."

And so God's providence works. Was the man human or angel? We are not to know for John never found out who gave him the money. But a few days after this act of kindness, a message came from the Countess of Richmond, inviting him to tutor her brother's children.

John Foxe stayed in England until Mary ascended to the British throne in 1553. Roman Catholicism was restored under her reign. He was, by this time, a noted Protestant whose writings and Lutheran views were well known. Although he kept out of the public eye as much as possible, his life was in jeopardy.

John moved his family to Frankfurt, Germany, and there he began to compile the commentary for which he was to become famous—*The Book of Martyrs*—the stories of those who suffered for the sake of Christ. He wrote between the drudgery of his job at proofreading for German printers. The job was taken so that he could provide bread, water and lodging for his family. He was wretchedly poor.

In August 1559, the first edition of *The Book of Martyrs* was run off. Comprising 750 pages, it was divided into six books. John and his family now travelled back to England, and when their feet touched British soil, Queen Elizabeth had been on the throne for about a year. One of John's former pupils provided him with a house and over the next fifteen years John proofread and edited for various printers.

John Foxe's gift was his writing. Friends and kinsfolk of sufferers told him their tales, and through John's book, they also tell us. John edited, rewrote and added to his chapters. In 1563, *The Book of Martyrs* was reprinted. It was about three times the size of the original version.

Foxe died in 1587, "not through any known disease, but through much age," wrote his son Simeon. He was seventy years old and was buried at St. Giles Cripplegate Church, in London, where he had often preached.

Food for thought

1. Do you think the devil might have had reasons for not wanting John Foxe to write? Why or why not?

2. Why do you think John Foxe wrote *The Book of Martyrs*?

19

Deuteronomy 6:4–9 *Hear, O Israel: The Lord our God, the Lord is one. You shall love the Lord your God with all your heart and with all your soul and with all your might. And these words that I command you today shall be on your heart. You shall teach them diligently to your children, and shall talk of them when you sit in your house, and when you walk by the way, and when you lie down, and when you rise. You shall bind them as a sign on your hand, and they shall be as frontlets between your eyes. You shall write them on the doorposts of your house and on your gates.*

God has appointed the press to preach

n 1396 a small baby, later baptized Johann Gensfleisch, was laid in his mother's arms by a midwife. Little did the hardworking wife of a German scribe, realize that the wailing baby she hushed would be used by God for a very special work—work which God had prepared in advance for him to do.

As a toddler, Johann probably took his first steps around his father's writing table. Cluttered with documents, this table was in a no-trespassing zone for the little one. But, soaked through with original sin, Johann crawled over from time to time, pulling himself up by his father's leg, and smiling winsomely. Having to copy much tedious work and being a patient man, his father lifted the little one onto his lap every now and then. Johan was sometimes thrown up into the air and briefly hugged for a moment before he was set down again.

It can be imagined that on one occasion his father, tired of monotonous work, let the boy stay on his lap a wee bit longer until little Johann, with an unexpected motion, made a sudden lunge for the inkwell. Black spots on white paper! Hours of painstaking and hard work spoiled! Johann might have laughed with delight at seeing the ink run, at the fanatic blotting his father would have attempted, and at the wonderful lines and figures he saw on the paper. It might have been the first, second or third time Johann was allowed near his father's writing table, but it most certainly would have been the last.

Growing up as a young lad, the boy did not often get his father's full attention. A scribe's work was never done. For hours on end, he was bent over his desk. The lighting was poor and the manuscripts intricate. Sometimes Johann was sent out to either deliver a finished one or to pick up a new one to be copied. Nobility, clergy and lawyers alike, all made ready use of his father's services. It is therefore easy to suppose that the young lad, loving his father, decided early on in his life that someday he would devise a tool to make writing easier. He thought a great deal about this as he lay in his bed at night and as he walked through the streets of Mainz, Germany.

Johann Gensfleisch took the name Gutenberg, probably his mother's maiden name, or the name of her birthplace, when he was older. He also began to experiment with what we now call the printing business. By the time he was twenty-eight, he had exhausted all his resources and was looking for financial backing so that he could continue. He worked with his shutters closed and his doors shut. The folks in Mainz, especially those attached to the scribe guilds, started rumours that young Johann, who was a devout Catholic, was an alchemist. But nothing deterred him.

By God's grace, Johann Gutenberg devised several techniques that remained basic to the printing industry until photo-processing, computerization, digital photography and such came along.

By 1449, when Johann was fifty-three, his finances were in dire straits. He approached a goldsmith, Johann Fust, wealthy and astute, and asked for a loan. As security, he pledged his entire printing operation. Fust knew a good thing when he saw it. He believed that if Johann Gutenberg could make the press succeed there would be much profit. He agreed to the loan and later, when Gutenberg ran out of funds again, he agreed to a second loan.

Peter Schöffer later joined the partnership that had by now formed between Fust and Gutenberg. A finished printing machine began printing and a Latin Bible rolled off the press. Fust's business acumen had been correct; profits began to come in. The Bible, known as the Gutenberg Bible—or the Mazarin Bible or the Forty-two Line Bible—was completed around 1455 or 1456. It was probably the earliest book printed on the new movable type press.

The relationship between Fust and Gutenberg, however, was not a good one. After the operation of the press appeared solid and sure, Fust sued Gutenberg for his money and, with the help of Schöffer, completely took over the printing shop. Gutenberg, the brains behind the whole set-up, was left without type and without a press. It is said that his name did not even appear on the title page of anything that he printed, most of which would have been religious, and neither was he allowed to retain even a small percentage of the profit.

Johann Gutenberg acquired a minor job with the Archbishop of Mainz, and died in 1468—a poor man who had been much taken advantage of. He was childless, friendless and practically unknown.

Food for thought

1. According to Deuteronomy 6:9, we are all involved in the writing business. It is certain that the devil, that wily old serpent, has also stained his nails with ink. Comment on this.

2. We live in an age where technology has advanced much beyond Gutenberg. How can we be accountable and use this technology (cellphones, computers, iPads), to God's glory and honour and to the advance of his kingdom?

20

Ecclesiastes 2:4–11 I made great works. I built houses and planted vineyards for myself. I made myself gardens and parks....I bought male and female slaves, and had slaves who were born in my house. I had also great possessions of herds and flocks....I also gathered for myself silver and gold and the treasure of kings and provinces. I got singers, both men and women, and many concubines, the delight of the sons of man. So I became great and surpassed all who were before me in Jerusalem. Also my wisdom remained with me. And whatever my eyes desired I did not keep from them. I kept my heart from no pleasure, for my heart found pleasure in all my toil, and this was my reward for all my toil. Then I considered all that my hands had done and the toil I had expended in doing it, and behold, all was vanity and a striving after wind, and there was nothing to be gained under the sun.

Grasping for the wind

A great many years ago, quite a few tribes occupied a country whose boundaries are the Carpathian mountains, the Oder and the Bug rivers and Prussia. That country is Poland. The Poles, however, are not an ancient people. Indeed, the word Pole is no older than the tenth century and seems to have indicated not so much the people of the area, as the region in which they lived. Polska, in the Slavonic tongue, means "level field" or "plain."

Before the ninth century, the Poles were a people of divided tribes—tribes independent of one another, each having a separate chief. Although in case of invasion these tribes might all pull together, most of the time they had little to do with each other.

It is said that during the 600s a man by the name of Leszek began clearing an area of land to build himself a house. As he was working the soil, he came across an eagle's nest. Consequently, he called the name of that place Gnesen, from the Slavonic word *gniazda*, nest. This is said to be why the Polish flag has an eagle on it. Leszek's home was eventually surrounded by other homes, and Gnesen was the capital of Poland for a few centuries. Leszek's descendants ruled for a while. At length, they were overthrown, and Poland began to have a succession of rulers. One of these, a man by the name of Cracus, was more powerful than the other rulers. He founded a city called Cracow, which surpassed Gnesen and took its place as capital. Although Cracus appears to have been a noble man, his two sons did not follow in his footsteps. In a struggle for power, one assassinated the other. When his crime came to light, however, the people banished him, and out of respect for Cracus, whom all had loved, they elevated his daughter, Wanda, to the throne.

Now Wanda was a beautiful girl. No doubt, having been the daughter of a powerful ruler all her life, she had been spoiled and quite adored. She was a headstrong, bright and ambitious girl who was convinced that to live was to rule—to be powerful. Not wanting to share her moment in history with anyone, and dusting off the throne for only one person, herself, she adamantly refused all offers of marriage. She had many who came to seek her hand. One of these was a German prince by the name of Rudiger. Offended and stung to the quick by her haughtiness, he was not willing to accept "no" to his offer of marriage. Mustering together a German army, he marched against Poland.

Wanda was not intimidated in the least, young woman though she was, and she boldly met his army at the head of her own army. When the two armies met, Rudiger again proposed in front of thousands of men, and was again spurned. Not giving up, he implored her to stop the shedding of innocent blood by becoming his wife, to which she responded by saying: "I will never become the slave of a husband, since, whoever he might be, will assuredly love me much less than my power."

For a moment Rudiger was tongue-tied. Meanwhile, Wanda's

answer spread like wildfire among Rudiger's troops. Then, amazingly enough, the entire German corps was filled with admiration for what they perceived to be courage in Poland's princess. They saw her riding from rank to rank as she spoke to her men, stimulating them to fight bravely in the oncoming battle. Convinced that opposition to Wanda would be a useless fight, they approached Rudiger and asked him what he could possibly gain by a battle.

"If you win," they said, "will she pardon you for the loss of her troops? And if you lose, will she love you?"

Rudiger refused to listen to his men and shouted that they should attack. His men, however, refused to obey. No matter how Rudiger urged them on, they stood without moving into battle. In utter despair, Rudiger finally ran himself through with his sword and as he lay dying, looked at the Polish camp.

Wanda did not mourn her would-be husband in the least. She returned in triumph to the capital city of Cracow.

Although Poland was evangelized in later centuries, at this point in time it was a pagan country. Wanda was a pagan queen. She did not worship God, but worshipped many gods. Not too long afterward, she sacrificed to idols in a heathen temple. She left the temple, dissatisfied with her life. Overcome by these feelings (and perhaps remorse), she made for the river Vistula. She stood for a while on the banks of this river, then she ended her life by throwing herself in the black waters, drowning almost immediately.

How sad when one has no purpose in life! How sad when, having come to the conclusion that money, power and prestige will not suffice, the only answer given is suicide! Both Wanda and Rudiger had been given much, but both failed to achieve the satisfaction of producing anything of eternal value.

Food for thought

1. What is your purpose in life? How do you act out this purpose in what you say and do?

2. How do people "chase after wind"?

21

Luke 23:39–43 *One of the criminals who were hanged railed at him, saying: "Are you the Christ? Save yourself and us!" But the other rebuked him, saying: "Do you not fear God, since you are under the same sentence of condemnation? And we indeed justly, for we are receiving the due reward of our deeds; but this man has done nothing wrong." And he said, "Jesus, remember me when you come into your kingdom." And he said to him, "Truly, I say to you, today you will be with me in Paradise."*

The other criminal

To be saved is never our own work. We cannot buy our salvation; we cannot perform a million good works and earn salvation; and neither can we with our prayers talk our way into heaven. There is only one way, and that way is through our Lord Jesus Christ. Sometimes Jesus reveals himself to a person in childhood; at other times, people come to know Jesus later in life, maybe even on their deathbed. So it was with a certain doctor.

A story is told by Rev. Hobson (1831–1914)—who ministered to a congregation in Liverpool—of a doctor who attended his church quite regularly. He came to the services, listened intently to the preaching, and appeared serious about his life and work. He did not, however, become a member.

"Doctor," Rev. Hobson felt impelled to say after some time, "are you born again?"

It is a question many are afraid to ask their fellow churchgoers and relatives, but it is a question which has eternal consequences.

"I cannot say I am," the doctor answered.

He was quiet for a moment before he went on.

"I had a very pious mother. Her prayers and influence probably kept me from drinking and other bad habits while I was going to school."

Rev. Hobson did not press the matter but rejoiced when soon afterward the doctor expressed a desire to join the church.

Then disaster visited the doctor's household. His eldest son, a very much beloved child, became ill. All the skills the doctor had acquired in school could do nothing for this child. No matter how he lavished medicine upon him, no matter how much he prayed, the boy grew weaker and weaker. And then one day, he died. Distraught the doctor wept and cried out. But nothing brought the child back.

Before the funeral, the doctor had "In Memoriam" cards printed at a print shop. On them he had printed two verses, very hopeful and glad verses. They were from John 11:25–26,: Jesus said... "I am the resurrection and the life. He who believes in Me will live, even though he dies; and whoever lives and believes in Me will never die. Do you believe this?"

These little cards were handed out and given to friends and relatives and fellow churchgoers. Rev. Hobson also received one.

The devil always tries to plant doubts in the hearts of believers. The doctor chanced to read a book shortly after the death of his little son. It made fun of Christianity and laughed at things like the seven-day Creation about which Genesis speaks. Influenced by a man named Darwin, the book said that science had all the answers and that Christians were quite foolish. The doctor pondered deeply. He had studied science in school, and he liked to prove things; he liked to see them with his eyes. Now when he went to church, he began to consider the things he heard childish and silly. The upshot of the matter was that he stopped attending, and was no longer a member.

Rev. Hobson, who loved the doctor, grieved for him. He resolved to pray for him, and in order to remember to pray for him, placed the little "In Memoriam" card with the comforting texts in his Bible. From time to time, he would meet the doctor in the street. The doctor would be carrying his black bag containing all the instruments he would need for a house call to some patient, and Rev. Hobson would be carrying his Bible containing the words of life.

"How are you, doctor?" Rev. Hobson would say as they stopped to chat.

"Very well," the doctor would answer, "I am just going out on a call."

"I am also going out," Rev. Hobson would answer, "and I would like you to know that I continue to keep you in my prayers."

The doctor smiled. He liked Rev. Hobson, whom he knew loved him. At this point, the pastor drew out the card and held it up.

"I keep it in my Bible, friend," he said, "as a reminder to pray for you. I have faith that one day you will be restored to the faith of your mother."

The doctor smiled politely.

"Well, your prayers will do no harm," he answered softly.

But the doctor's face had a lean, hungry look—a look that said he was not happy. Over the next ten years, the two met frequently in the streets of Liverpool. Always when they met, Rev. Hobson would draw out the card with the texts to remind the doctor of the prayers being offered in his behalf.

One day, as they met in the street, after shaking hands and exchanging trivialities, Rev. Hobson posed the same question to the doctor that he had asked him so many years earlier.

"Doctor," he said, "do you now believe in God?"

A tremor passed over the doctor's face. He looked down at the ground for a long moment and then looked up full into the pastor's face.

"Yes, I do," he answered.

"Do you also believe in Jesus?"

"I do," he responded and smiled.

Not long afterward, the doctor became ill. Rev. Hobson visited him in his home. It was a serious illness, and it appeared obvious that the man, not yet old, would soon die. In the presence of his family, with tears in his eyes, the doctor asked Rev. Hobson if he would be so good as to conduct his funeral.

"As a Christian?" Rev. Hobson asked.

"Yes, as a Christian," the doctor answered.

The doctor died and, even as the thief on the cross, went to Paradise. And we who are left behind ought to pray—pray for all the doctors we know whom we pass in the street.

Food for thought

1. Do you know anyone who, like the doctor, professes not to believe what he or she has grown up with? How do you treat this person? Should you tell this person what Rev. Hobson told the doctor?

2. God is gracious and merciful. How is this illustrated in the life of the other thief, the criminal who was forgiven by Jesus at the last moment in his life?

22

Proverbs 24:26 *Whoever gives an honest answer kisses the lips.*

Greeting one another with a holy kiss

Honesty's the best policy. So goes the saying anyway. As a matter of fact, a person would be admitting his own dishonesty if he disagreed with that saying. "An honest man's the noblest work of God," said Alexander Pope. Yes, trust, truthfulness, reliability and all those virtues are wonderful, and Christians should strive to practice them.

However, we like to bend the truth a little when it suits our purposes. One of the mildest and most innocent forms of this is the joke. Exaggeration, tall tales and the twisting of facts often cause chuckles as in the following story.

Two musicians were discussing a mutual friend.

"It was terrible, just terrible about Maurice," said the first.

"What happened?"

"He was playing in a concert and his toupee fell into his French horn."

"Yes, I can understand that he would be embarrassed, but is it really that terrible?"

"The accident, no. It was the review all the papers carried that was so awful."

"What review?"

"The one that said that Maurice spent the whole evening blowing his top."

A bit of laughter is fine. It is good medicine. And when we tell a joke, those who listen are aware, usually, that what we say is in fun, and that our words can be taken with a grain of salt.

"Truth is the most valuable thing we have," said Mark Twain, "Let us economize on it." Many people do just that. There are many stories of those in power who have lied over the years.

There is a story, a true one, by the way, of a man in Scotland who did tell the truth and who was blessed by doing so.

For many years an old building, two stories high with a thatched roof, stood in the city of Sanquhar, Scotland. Built in the 1500s and rebuilt in 1735, it was known as the tolbooth. In a state of disrepair, this building was multi-functional. It served as tolbooth, council house, court and prison all in one. Affixed to an outside wall was an upright iron bar with a strong iron ring. This was an instrument of punishment known as the "jougs." It resembled the English pillory and stocks and was used for the punishment of thieves. An iron chain attached to the ring encircled the neck of the prisoner and was securely fastened by a padlock. When the thief was tied in, anyone who passed could throw what they thought fitted the crime: rotten eggs, over-ripe tomatoes and any other garbage.

In the late 1800s, a man by the name of William Stitt was imprisoned in the tolbooth in the section of the building known as the debtor's prison. He had been unfortunate enough to fall into the hands of an unmerciful creditor. William Stitt, in other words, owed money and could not pay. Although the prison cells accorded to debtors were cold and miserable, William Stitt did not suffer badly when he was first incarcerated. It was, you see, summertime. However, as the months passed and William stayed in prison, fall changed to winter. Temperatures dropped sharply. Because the authorities in charge of the tolbooth were extremely sparing with blankets, William ran a good chance of either catching pneumonia or freezing to death.

William, a reflective man, thought of the warm blankets his mother had at home, and knew she would be more than willing to let him borrow some. Therefore, he decided to go and get them. Managing somehow to force his way through a sky-light window, he ended up on the roof. Once there, he descended to the street by jumping on top of the shed of an old smithy which leaned against the tolbooth wall. When his feet touched the cobblestones, William smiled and happily began to jog his way to the village of Durisdeer where his mother lived. When he knocked at her door in the dead of night she was startled, but recovering her wits she was more than happy to furnish her son with some of the coveted blankets.

When the jailer came into work early the next morning, keys dangling from his belt, he found William Stitt standing at the door, a bundle of blankets draped over his arm.

"What are you doing?" he bellowed to the outside inmate.

"The nichts were gie cauld," answered William "an' I thocht I wad be daein' nae harm, an' never be missed sud I step awa hame for some claes to keep meself warm." (The nights were getting cold, and I thought I would be doing no harm and never be missed should I step away home for some clothes to keep myself warm.)

By this time the jailer had the door open and, pushing the offender through, ushered him back into the cell. Needless to say, William slept warmly and soundly the next night.

When William's creditor heard of the escapade, he was very impressed. Refusing to press further charges, he dismissed the debt, and William was set free. Had he not returned to jail to face his obligations, he would have been a wanted man, hunted by the authorities. As it stood, he was rewarded for his honesty.

Food for thought

1. "Whoever gives an honest answer kisses the lips" says Proverbs 24:26. Can we greet one another with honesty? Look up texts such as Romans 16:16; 1 Corinthians 16:20; 2 Corinthians 13:12; 1 Thessalonians 5:26 and 1 Peter 5:14. Can you think of an incident in the Bible where the most deceitful kiss was given?

2. How can a person economize on the truth?

23

Proverbs 31:10–12 *An excellent wife who can find? She is far more precious than jewels. The heart of her husband trusts in her, and he will have no lack of gain. She does him good, and not harm, all the days of her life.*

Her price is Sheol

You can paraphrase the Proverbs 31:10–12 quote to conversely read: *A virtuous mistress, who can find? She is worthless. The heart of her lover safely trusts her but he will have no gain. She does him evil and not good all the days of her life.* This converse quote is acted out in the life of Henry II of France. Listen to a bit of his life and judge for yourself.

Henry II ascended to the throne with much pomp and splendour in 1547. During the coronation festivities, four Huguenots were selected to be burnt at the stake. One of these was a poor tailor. He was poor only, however, in material goods for he was a child of God and delighted in that. Thinking to give the would-be king some entertainment, the bishops thought that the little tailor would make good sport in the royal apartment for all the nobles prior to his execution. So he was taken from the prison to the splendid rooms of Henry and his entourage.

It was a shameful encounter. Everyone mocked the tailor. They reviled him. But throughout it all, the man stood calm and secure. Despite his humble station, he was able to make intelligent and honourable replies, so that the tongues of all those present were ashamed and stilled. All tongues, that is, but that of the king's mistress, whose name was Diana of Poitiers. She was irritated that such a small person, a man of such little consequence, in her estimation, should silence the court. She stepped forward and began to ridicule him and his faith in an arrogant manner. But he was not the least intimidated by her rich gown, nor by her imperious tone.

"Be satisfied, Madame," he said, without any regard for her position as Henry's favourite, "with having infected France, without mingling your venom and filth in a matter as altogether holy and sacred, as is the religion and truth of our Lord Jesus Christ."

This personal affront to his mistress was too much for Henry II, and he ordered the tailor taken from his presence.

July 14, 1549, was the day when the tailor was to burn. Henry II was seated at a window which gave him a particularly close and advantageous view of the stake. He sat down next to Diana of Poitiers and prepared to enjoy himself. To his satisfaction, he saw the tailor bound and with a grim smile he watched the faggots kindled. But then a curious thing happened. The tailor, upon turning his head toward the window, saw the king with his mistress seated at his side. From that moment on, the tailor never looked away from his earthly monarch. He gazed at the king unwaveringly, his eyes serious and condemning. At first Henry stared back, unafraid. But as time wore on and the little tailor kept staring and staring, he became uncomfortable. He stood up and wandered about the apartment, but then, as if drawn by some invisible cord, he was pulled back to his chair. And always the man was still looking, always looking at him. Even when the flames blazed around his face, the tailor's eyes, not vacillating for a moment, burned into Henry's soul.

When the execution was over, the king was upset. He had night-mares that night and neither Diana of Poitiers' sultry eyes nor her passionate embraces, alleviated his fears. Henry II saw the martyr's eyes everywhere, and many times that night and the following night, he sat up in a sweat trying to assuage his conscience. He consequently took an oath that he would never again attend an execution.

Persecution of the Huguenots remained common during Henry's reign. Diana's greed, for often Henry would give her the estates of martyrs, was insatiable. She goaded him to sanction many burnings. It is of interest to note that toward the end of his reign, he called an assembly in which he urged his senators to adopt new and even stricter measures against the Huguenots.

Two weeks after this assembly, Henry attended a tournament. Diana of Poitiers was at his side. While jousting, Henry was involved in an accident, that is to say, an "act of God." A lance struck his visor with such force that it flew open, and splinters pierced his eye. Ten days later, in his forty-first year, Henry II was no more. His earthly reign was over.

Food for thought

1. Henry II's casket was covered with a tapestry that had the words "Saul, Saul, why persecutest thou Me?" embroidered on it. What are your thoughts on that?

2. Although at the time perhaps one might have preferred to be the king rather than the tailor, with regard to the death the tailor had to die, reflect on where both are today?

24

Hebrews 11:13 *These all died in faith, not having received the things promised, but having seen them and greeted them from afar, and having acknowledged that they were strangers and exiles on the earth.*

We have no hearth

Before a hostile court at Wigtown, Scotland, on April 13, 1685, stood several female prisoners. Their crime was that they had refused the Oath of Abjuration—an oath which made the swearer confess that the church of God was a mere department of the state. The women who had refused to swear were accused of rebellion for attending worship meetings with like-minded people. As it was ruled that they were guilty, the judge ordered that they should kneel to the court as they received their sentences.

Today it is a small thing for twenty-first-century Christians to kneel to the world. Nevertheless, these particular 1685 women would not do such a small thing as kneel down while receiving sentence from a judge, although it might be argued that kneeling would not compromise their faith.

Brutally held down by soldiers, they received their sentences. Margaret MacLachlan, widow, seventy years of age, to die by drowning; Margaret Maxwell, serving maid, twenty years of age, to be flogged publicly through the streets of Wigtown three days in succession and to stand each of these days for an hour in the stocks; Margaret Wilson, eighteen years of age, to die by drowning; Agnes Wilson, sister of Margaret, thirteen years of age, whose father would have to pay £100 pounds to buy her freedom.

Margaret Wilson and Margaret MacLachlan were both taken to the banks of Blednoch Burn which fills up from the sea when the swift running tide comes in. Two long wooden stakes had been fixed deeply in the bed of the burn. The farther one out was for the older woman. The nearer one was reserved for the younger.

At this point, all either Margaret had to do was affirm the oath. It required only one small sentence and they would have been physically free. But there was the matter of witness. There were the children and grandchildren watching. The old Margaret looked at them and would not say a word to the soldiers. She merely spoke to the Lord in prayer. The waves lapped her up, and the soldiers laughed until she choked in the swirling water.

Then young Margaret Maxwell was asked if she would reconsider. Pointing to the limp body of the old Margaret the soldiers said, "What do you think of her now?"

She answered clearly, and all those watching heard her.

"I see Christ wrestling there. Do you think that she and I are sufferers? No, it is Christ in us, for he sends no warfare at his own charges."

The waters began rising around the young Margaret, and she began to sing a song she had learned during worship.

Then, having been permitted to hold on to her Bible, she opened it to Romans 8 and read out loud:

For I am persuaded that neither death nor life, nor angels, nor principalities, nor powers, nor things present, nor things to come, nor height, nor depth, nor any other creature, shall be able to separate us from the love of God, which is in Christ Jesus our Lord.

At this point the soldiers, because of her youth and because they had been moved in spite of themselves, took the ropes off young Margaret's body and pulled her to shore.

"Pray for the king," they enjoined her, meaning Charles II of England, "as he is supreme over all persons and causes, ecclesiastic as well as civil."

She looked at them, physically weak but fully clothed with the armour of God.

"I wish the salvation of all and the damnation of none," she whispered in response.

They dunked her and pleaded with her to give in. But she had just seen a mother in Israel die and ascend to heaven. She had been trained and knew which way to go. She had just read a most encouraging word from the Lord, and she knew for a fact, that nothing could separate her from him.

"Lord, give the king repentance, forgiveness and salvation, if it be thy holy will," she said, her dress sodden, damp and clinging to her body coldly.

"The oath, Margaret!"

The soldiers were angry. She groaned.

"No sinful oath for me. I am one of Christ's children. Let me go."

And they tied her to the stake again where she soon joined the older Margaret in eternal glory.

O LORD, my heart is not lifted up; my eyes are not raised too high; I do not occupy myself with things too great and too marvelous for me. But I have calmed and quieted my soul, like a weaned child with its mother; like a weaned child is my soul within me (Psalm 131:1–2).

Food for thought

1. Many times women are underpaid and segregated. The cry is that women ought to stand up and fight for themselves. Careers, money and a place in society are what counts. Would you have wanted one of the Margarets for a mother or sister? Why?

2. Would you fit the description of the pilgrim saints that the poet Delta Moir wrote about?

> We have no hearth—the ashes lie
> In blackness where they brightly shone;
> We have no home—the desert sky
> Our covering, th'earth couch alone;
> We have no heritage—depriven
> Of these, we ask not such on earth;
> Our hearts are sealed; we seek in heaven
> For heritage, and home and hearth.

If so, why or why not?

25

Isaiah 55:1–2 *Come, everyone who thirsts, come to the waters; and he who has no money, come, buy and eat! Come, buy wine and milk without money and without price. Why do you spend your money for that which is not bread, and your labor for that which does not satisfy? Listen diligently to me, and eat what is good, and delight yourselves in rich food.*

What is not bread

Almost 500 years ago, around the time of the Reformation, tickets were produced and run off by the millions stamped with the pope's personal stamp of forgiveness. For a mere handful of coins, for a tract of land, actually for whatever a person was willing to offer, a pardon for sins committed in the past or in the future could be bought. These tickets, called indulgences, were thought to be handy to have around in case of accidental death, illness leading to death or prior to a well-thought-out burglary.

The sale of indulgences in Switzerland was assigned by Rome to a smooth-talking cordelier by the name of Bernardin Samson. (A cordelier was a Franciscan friar, so called because of a knotted cord worn as a girdle around his waist.) Samson had already proved his character to several popes by outselling a host of other friars. He had transported many chests filled with gold and silver vessels back to Rome, as well as innumerable bags of coins.

In every town in Switzerland, Samson set up his stalls. People from all walks of life begged to purchase indulgences. Samson was ingenious in devising ways and means so that even the poorest of the poor could afford his luxury. He advertised three different kinds of indulgences. The very rich might buy one for a sum of approximately $500; whereas the middle class could obtain an indulgence for $1 and the poor could get away with paying "two batzen," that is to say, about three-halfpence. But if someone had no money to speak of, and Samson's eye fell upon a piece of property, or say a horse, he was not averse to striking a bargain.

As he travelled through many different towns, Samson's chests began to grow heavier and heavier. But in the city of Baden, he finally met his match. And a fool with a child's heart set him right.

At first, business was brisk in Baden. Many people felt the need for an indulgence; many people felt the weight of their guilt and wanted to be assured of heaven. As he had done in the previous town he had visited, Samson made what he deemed to be a most generous statement. "All the souls of Baden," he echoed across the Baden square, "who are dead, whatever may have been the manner or the place of their death, are delivered from the torments of purgatory and of hell."

Many people cheered. Encouraged by these fans, Samson felt inspired to say more. And so he did after conducting Mass. He formed a procession, put himself at its head and marched around the churchyard while chanting the office for the dead. Suddenly stopping, he gazed into the sky and spoke again.

"Ecce volant!" he cried in a majestic voice ("See how they fly!"). He meant, and everyone did seem to follow him, that the souls of those in purgatory were escaping from purgatory and were flying over Baden's cemetery on their way to Paradise. Everyone looked up at the sky. There was nothing to be seen. It was a clear sky with just the smallest hint of a breeze stirring the leaves of the trees.

The Baden fool, a harmless soul and tolerated by all, grinned to himself as he stared upward with the crowd. And grinning still, while everyone mindlessly kept gazing up, he climbed the stairs of the Baden steeple taking with him a bag of feathers. Then, merrily waving to everyone below, he emptied the bag.

"Ecce volant!" he cried and laughed, "See how they fly!"

The spell was broken. Suddenly everyone seemed to realize the ludicrousness of the situation and laughter began. First only a few people guffawed, but soon the whole crowd rocked with hilarity.

Samson was livid. He saw that he had lost his hold over his audience and that this episode might hamper the sale of future indulgences.

"Seize that man," he ordered, pointing up at the fool.

But the townsfolk, although indulgent to the point of buying indulgences for what they believed was their rightful due (eternal salvation), would not indulge the monk in this.

"He is a harmless soul," they said to Samson as they grinned, "a half-wit."

They would not lay a hand on the man, and indulgence sales dropped drastically.

After Samson left Switzerland, carrying with him numerous coffers filled with the money of those who desired to buy salvation, the plague struck that country. It spread from city to city, through valley after valley, and killed many. Ravaging the countryside, inflicting dreadful losses to every family, perhaps some people felt safe fingering that little piece of paper which they felt to be their passport to salvation. But it is more likely that most people felt cheated, for the paper gave them no comfort in time of need—none at all.

Food for thought

1. Is harbouring a slogan such as "You are number one" or "Freedom fifty-five" an indulgence? Why or why or why not?

2. Do you feel just a slight bit of self-righteousness about attending two

church services every Sunday or about tithing? Explain in your own words how you feel about these things and why.

26

Revelation 1:4 *Grace to you and peace from him who is and who was and who is to come, and from the seven spirits who are before his throne, and from Jesus Christ, the faithful witness, the firstborn of the dead, and the ruler of kings on earth.*

One of the kings

Born in Saint-Germain-en-Laye, France, on September 5, 1638, the cherub-faced baby was regarded as somewhat of a miracle by his parents. Louis Bourbon, also known as Louis XIII, and Anne of Austria, had already been married twenty-three years when he arrived. Perhaps it set the stage for spoiling the child who would later be known as the Sun King.

The boy, who became Louis XIV, lived a life that was well-recorded. At the age of two, for example, he showed a pronounced dislike for his father, ate with his fingers and was fond of peas. As he grew older, he developed a particular aversion for two things: baths and books. In early manhood, Louis began to wear six-inch heels to make him appear taller than his five-foot four-inch height; he also generally changed his clothes three times a day (no wonder, what with his aversion to baths!); and, because his father and mother did not employ the biblical tactics for shepherding a child's heart, he developed into the epitome of selfishness.

Louis, indulged by all, ascended to the throne of France at the tender age of five, his mother being regent during his minority. Cardinal Jules Mazarin cared for the administration of the kingdom, and when he died early on in Louis' reign, he left the young boy king the wealthiest, most powerful ruler in Europe.

Little compassion beat in Louis' royal heart. When someone called attention to the hunger misery in the country during the famine in the winter of 1709, he said "and what if thousands of those scoundrels die, since they are useful for nothing? Would France be less France?" Louis persecuted the Protestants for most of his adult life. He was very cruel and used measures later copied by Hitler. Dragoons sacked towns, tortured families, hung men and women by their feet, burned them over wet hay and threw them into wells. It's no wonder that some 200,000 to 300,000 escaped to friendlier countries.

Louis XIV died on September 1, 1715. Humanly speaking, he had reigned long; presided over a magnificent court; achieved intellectual and artistic success; won a number of military battles. He also left behind unrivalled extravagance and monetary bankruptcy.

The month prior to his death, Louis still walked through his well-tended garden on his high heels, supervising placement of marble statues. He over-ate at dinners and had no lack of courtiers who fawned over him. The sciatica that hit him rather suddenly, put him into bed and a dozen or so courtiers stood at his bedside as he moaned, groaned and complained. His last days, as all his other days, were public. Doctors purged him, bled him and had him take baths in silver bathtubs filled with donkey's milk mixed with Burgundy wine. Italian musicians played soothing motets as he soaked. The doctors ignored his real physical problem, a gangrenous leg, and the king himself was rather dubious as he sat in his bath.

"Do you really think this will help me?" he asked his physicians.

Having some inkling of impending death, he sent for and pedantically spoke to his priest confessor, sadly declaring that he was not suffering enough for the expiation of his sins. As he sat in a wheelchair, his gangrenous leg on a stool, he also addressed the many cardinals who had swarmed to his bedside. He vehemently avowed that the responsibility for his religious policies was theirs and that his conscience was clear before God since he had only followed their orders.

On August 27, 1715, two weeks after becoming ill, Maréchal, the royal surgeon, operated on Louis' gangrenous leg.

"Ah, Maréchal, how you are hurting me!" he cried and four days later, surgery notwithstanding, he was dead.

The day after he died, Maréchal opened the body, removed the heart and intestines and performed an autopsy. The body was embalmed and placed in a lead casket. The lead casket was then placed in a thick oak coffin and sealed with iron bands. A copper plate nailed to the oak coffin read:

This is the body of the very high and very powerful prince Louis XIV, called the great, of the family of the house of Bourbon, King of France and Navarre, deceased in Versailles the first of September 1715 at the age of 77 years, and born in Saint-Germaine-en-Laye, September 5, 1638. He reigned 72 years, 3 months and 18 days.

Food for thought

1. All the fuss over his funeral did not keep Louis XIV from his appointment with the Ruler of the kings of the earth, also known as the Alpha and Omega. His time on the earth had been a mere royal drop in the bucket when weighed against God's eternity. Comment.

2. Louis had access to the law and the prophets. More than that, he had access to Jesus Christ, the fulfilment of Old Testament law and prophecy. Had he repented, would he have been forgiven even in his

gangrenous old age? Read 2 Chronicles 33:1–13 to refresh your memory on the reign of wicked King Manasseh.

27

Psalm 45:1,17 *My heart overflows with a pleasing theme; I address my verses to the King; my tongue is like the pen of a ready scribe...I will cause your name to be remembered in all generations; therefore nations will praise you forever and ever.*

A constant victory—a page in the life of Amy Carmichael
PART 1

Amy Carmichael was born in Millisle, Northern Ireland, in 1867. Her father was a flour miller and her mother a doctor's daughter. She was the firstborn and in due time became eldest sister to six more children.

Having no inclination whatsoever toward having a model childhood, Amy often encouraged her brothers and sisters in things they should not be doing. On one occasion, she suggested they all eat laburnum pods. She knew these pods were poisonous and thought it would be interesting to observe how long it would take to die. But parents have ways of finding these things out and before anything dreadful could happen, all the children were given a powerful emetic. Heaving as they vomited, all six siblings shot baleful glances at their eldest sister.

Another time, Amy led her small brothers through the skylight onto the roof. Sliding down into the gutters, they were having a marvelous time until they met, as all bad children's eyes eventually meet, their parents' eyes.

It was not only her brothers and sisters who were nudged into disobedience by Amy. She herself records a story of her schooldays,

> It was the year of the 1882 comet... The girls in my dormitory and I also wanted to see it. I was always the one sent to ask for favours.... So now I was sent to Miss Kay, the Principal, to ask her to allow us to sit up and see the comet. And she said, "Certainly not." Well, it was all wrong, but I tied threads to the great toes of the girls and held the ends of the threads, and promised to keep awake and pull those threads when everyone in the house was asleep...I pulled the threads...we stole softly, oh so softly, up the stairs to the attic from whose window we knew that the comet could be seen. And all the stairs creaked. And when we got there what do you think we saw? We saw the principal and teachers; they were looking at the comet. We looked at it too. We had time to see it beautifully before anyone had recovered sufficiently from the shock of our arrival to order us back to bed. That was a woeful night for me. I was sure I would be expelled and that would break my parents' hearts. Happily that did not come to pass.

Mr. and Mrs. Carmichael were Scottish Presbyterians and brought their children up to obey and respect the Lord. But it was not until Amy was seventeen that she really comprehended what obedience and respect to God would mean. She wrote:

> It was a dull Sunday morning in a street in Belfast.... My brothers and sisters and I were returning with our mother from church when we met a poor, pathetic old woman who was carrying a heavy bundle. We had never seen such a thing in Presbyterian Belfast on Sunday, and, moved by sudden

pity, my brothers and I turned with her, relieved her of the bundle, took her by her arms as though they had been handles, and helped her along. This meant facing all the respectable people who were, like ourselves, on their way home. It was a horrid moment. We were only two boys and a girl, and not at all exalted Christians. We hated doing it. Crimson all over (at least we felt crimson, soul and body of us) we plodded on, a wet wind blowing us about, and blowing, too, the rags of that poor old woman, till she seemed like a bundle of feathers and we unhappily mixed up with them. But just as we passed a fountain...this mighty phrase was suddenly flashed as it were through the grey drizzle: "Gold, silver, precious stones, wood, hay, stubble—every man's work shall be made manifest: for the day shall declare it, because it shall be revealed by fire; and the fire shall try every man's work of what sort it is. If any man's work abide."

"If any man's work abide" I turned to see the voice that spoke with me. The fountain, the muddy street, the people with their politely surprised faces, all this I saw, but nothing else. The blinding flash had come and gone...I knew that something had happened that had changed life's values. Nothing could ever matter again but the things that were eternal.

After this, Amy Carmichael began Bible classes for the poor girls of Belfast who were known as "shawlies"—girls who wore shawls because they could not afford hats. Her work was so blessed by the Lord that a hall was needed for the five-hundred women who came out regularly.

Food for thought

1. Like Amy Carmichael perhaps you were brought up by parents who taught you Christian values, who took you to church and told you it was proper to pray and read Scripture. Is knowledge of Jesus the same as knowing him personally? Why or why not?

2. James 1:22 says, "But be doers of the Word, and not hearers only, deceiving yourselves." How can you deceive yourself by only hearing the Word and not doing it?

28

1 Corinthians 3:11–17 *For no one can lay a foundation other than that which is laid, which is Jesus Christ. Now if anyone builds on the foundation with gold, silver, precious stones, wood, hay, straw—each one's work will become manifest, for the Day will disclose it, because it will be revealed by fire, and the fire will test what sort of work each one has done. If the work that anyone has built on the foundation survives, he will receive a reward. If anyone's work is burned up, he will suffer loss, though he himself will be saved, but only as through fire. Do you not know that you are God's temple and that God's Spirit dwells in you? If anyone destroys God's temple, God will destroy him. For God's temple is holy, and you are that temple.*

A constant victory—a page in the life of Amy Carmichael
PART 2

In 1895, Amy sailed to India as a missionary. Tamil was the language that had to be conquered. It was a difficult language and she had to study hard. Perhaps the words were not applicable, but she derived comfort from Numbers 22:28 which read: "The Lord opened the mouth of the donkey."

Amy learned the language and was gifted in her single desire to serve only the Lord. Greatly troubled by temple prostitution, she began to focus on helping children. Little girls were sometimes given, sometimes sold, by their families to temples. Trained in music and dancing, they were tortured if they tried to escape and taught to become prostitutes. A description of prostitution by one Hindu woman read:

> It is very meritorious to give a child to the gods. Often the parents are poor but of good Caste.... If the child is old enough to miss her mother, she is very carefully watched until she has forgotten her. Sometimes she is shut up into the back part of the house and punished....The punishment is severe enough to frighten the child.... Sometimes it is brandishment with a hot iron upon a place which does not show.... As soon as she can understand she is taught all evil and trained to think it is good.

The children that fled from this sickening practice were brought to Amy, whose name gradually changed to Amma—the Tamil for mother. Christian Indian women joined Amma in her work. The Dohnavur Fellowship was born—a fellowship of volunteer labourers. There were no salaried workers. No one was permitted to ask for money and needs were mentioned only to the Lord. Prayer was of primary importance. Amma felt India was a sleeping giant in Satan's grip who could not be awakened except by prayer. And so it was that every day, from 5 A.M. until 10 P.M. different people at the Fellowship prayed. There was a constant vigil.

Over the years, the Fellowship grew. Amma loved the children who were brought to her and sorely grieved when one of them died. On the death of one of these children, she wrote:

> Her name was Lulla. She was five years old, a Brahman child of much promise. She had sickened suddenly with an illness which we knew from the first must be dangerous.... We sent an urgent message to a medical evangelist trained at Neyyoor...and he came at once. He arrived an hour too late.... But before he came we had seen this...The child was in pain, struggling for breath, turning to us for what we could not give. I left...going to a side room, cried to our Father to take her quickly. I was not more than a minute away, but when I returned she was radiant. Her little lovely face was lighted with amazement and happiness. She was looking up

and clapping her hands as delighted children do. When she saw me she stretched out her arms and flung them around my neck as though saying goodbye, in a hurry to be gone; then she turned to the others in the same eager way, and then again, holding out her arms to Someone whom we could not see, she clapped her hands. Had only one of us seen this thing, we might have doubted. But we all three saw it. There was no trace of pain on her face. She was never to taste of pain again. We saw nothing in that dear child's face but unimaginable delight. We looked where she was looking, almost thinking that we should see what she saw.

One day a young man once came to Dohnavur to be instructed in Bible knowledge before his baptism. He was asked to help out around the compound.

"I did not come to work. I came to learn about baptism," he said, much offended. His young face turned with aversion from the patch of gravel he had been asked to weed. The task had been given him chiefly because it was in the shade of the house, a place of quiet, cool and comfort. A strong lad of nineteen or twenty, he had been sent by a fellow missionary. The boy had rested and had been fed for two full days, after a not very arduous journey, when Amma suggested that he do a little work.

"Don't you want to help? See, we are all at work."

"I did not come to work."

"But what about St. Paul? He laboured with his own hands. And what about our Lord Jesus? He worked as a carpenter."

"I did not come to work."

"The Bible says that if any will not work, neither shall he eat."

He ignored that remark and finally said that a Christian back home would support him.

"But she has paid your travelling expenses and helped you in other ways already. Isn't that enough?"

In the end, he left for other Christians who indulged him. He sat around, ate and learned and was baptized, and Dohnavur was sent the message: "Is that the way to treat a convert?"

Amma was convinced that it was. From their nursery days on, she demanded that her children learn that the reward of good work is not pay but the satisfaction of pleasing and honouring God.

Food for thought

1. Do you know any "sleeping giants" that cannot be awakened except by prayer? What are they? How much time do you and your church spend in prayer with regard to "sleeping giants"?

2. How do you feel about asking the Lord for money? Why do you feel this way?

29

Proverbs 21:1–3 *The king's heart is a stream of water in the hand of the Lord; he turns it wherever he will. Every way of a man is right in his own eyes, but the Lord weighs the heart. To do righteousness and justice is more acceptable to the Lord than sacrifice.*

A slice of Russian history

In the year A.D. 988 a pagan Russian ruler, Vladimir, was baptized in the Dnieper River. He consequently made Christianity (the Greek Orthodox kind), the state religion. On the day of his baptism he married Anna, daughter of the Byzantine emperor Romanos II.

Vladimir's conversion is said to have come about in a rather unique way. In 988 he besieged the Greek town of Kherson. Not able to break down its resistance, he resolved to persist even if it took until his dying day. His troops were arranged in battle formation and commanded to build a trench around the city. As they were busy digging, a citizen of Kherson shot an arrow from the wall on which was inscribed:

> To the east of thee lie springs, the waters of which come into town through pipes; dig there and thou shalt intercept the water.

When Vladimir was shown the arrow and the words inscribed on it, he was amazed. Having heard of the grandeur and beauty of the Greek religion, he vowed that if the inscription on the arrow was true, he would become a Christian. The soldiers were ordered to dig by the springs. The pipes were discovered and the water was cut off. Shortly afterward the people of Kherson, due to a lack of water, surrendered to Vladimir.

Vladimir kept his impetuous vow. When he returned home, carrying certain "sacred vessels" and "relics" with him from Greece, he built a church in the middle of Kiev. The church site was raised with the earth taken from the trench around Kherson. Not content with having a church building, Vladimir next ordered all idols in Kiev to be thrown out, chopped up and burned. Then, also wishing his subjects to be like-minded, he made the following proclamation:

> Whosoever tomorrow, rich or poor, mendicant or artisan, does not come to the river Dnieper to be baptized, will be as an alien to me.

Vladimir's people assumed that "might made right." They reasoned among themselves that if this new religion had given their ruler victory, it might not be a bad religion to embrace. When Vladimir came to the river the next day, together with his wife and some priests, multitudes had assembled there. These people had very little, if any, understanding of God. But the people,

> went into the water, some up to their necks, others to their breasts; the younger ones stood on the banks, men held their children in their arms, the adults were quite in the water, and the priests stood repeating the prayers.

Vladimir, happy to see so many of his people baptized, as he himself now was, next ordered that churches and priests be established in all other Russian towns and that their inhabitants should be baptized also.

Many of the radical changes in Vladimir's life, after his rather "un"orthodox conversion, were good. Prior to his conversion he had maintained several harems with hundreds of wives and concubines. Vladimir now put all these away and became the faithful husband of only one—Anna. Having murdered his brother in a power struggle eight years before, as well as having killed the father and brother of another one of his wives, he now became a fearful administrator of justice and abolished capital punishment lest he commit sin. He did, however, continue to wage full-fledged warfare during the remaining twenty-seven years of his reign.

At Vladimir's death in 1015, Russia had three bishoprics. He himself was later canonized by the Greek Orthodox Church and is remembered in the annals of Russian history as Saint Vladimir the Great. Although obviously not fully instructed in the principles of biblical Christianity, his acceptance of it did bring about a providential change in the Russian concept of many heathen gods over against the one true God.

Food for thought

1. Can you think of other instances in history where God has used a ruler to further his kingdom? Can you think of instances today?

2. Comment on Proverbs 21:2, "Every way of a man is right in his own eyes, but the Lord weighs the heart."

30

Ecclesiastes 9:16–18 *But I say that wisdom is better than might, though the poor man's wisdom is despised and his words are not heard. The words of the wise heard in quiet are better than the shouting of a ruler among fools. Wisdom is better than weapons of war, but one sinner destroys much good.*

Wisdom is better than weapons of war

The story of Sheba, a rebel during King David's reign, is fairly well known. Trying to muster up men to follow him in his rebellion and not getting enough support, Sheba fled to the city of Abel of Beth-maacah to hide from commander Joab. Joab surrounded the city, battered the wall, and was almost ready to annihilate it when a wise woman asked if she might speak with him. He complied and she said:

"Are you Joab?" He answered, "I am." Then she said to him, "Listen to the words of your servant." And he answered, "I am listening." Then she said, "They used to say in former times, 'Let them but ask counsel at Abel,' and so they settled a matter. I am one of those who are peaceable and faithful in Israel. You seek to destroy a city that is a mother in Israel. Why will you swallow up the heritage of the Lord?" Joab answered, "Far be it from me, far be it, that I should swallow up or destroy! That is not true. But a man of the hill country of Ephraim, called Sheba the son of Bichri, has lifted up his hand against King David. Give up him alone, and I will withdraw from the city." And the woman said to Joab, "Behold, his head shall be thrown to you over the wall." Then the woman went to all the people in her wisdom. And they cut off the head of Sheba the son of Bichri and threw it out to Joab. So he blew the trumpet, and they dispersed from the city, every man to his home. And Joab returned to Jerusalem to the king (2 Samuel 20:17–22).

So reads the chronicle of Sheba's demise, and so is recorded the wisdom of a woman in 2 Samuel 20. A great deal of bloodshed was averted both by this counsel of wisdom and by acting upon it. "Wisdom," Ecclesiastes 9:18 tells us, "is better than weapons of war." Indeed, there are several vignettes in history that bear this out.

During the Middle Ages, the city of Franeker in Friesland, a province in northern Netherlands, was besieged by enemies. Weeks grew into months, and the people inside the city grew hungrier and more desperate by the hour. There were arguments within homes. Mothers wept, and fathers were obdurate. Was it worthwhile to open the gate and let the marauder in and hope that some might escape the brutality that usually accompanied a victory? Agreement on this topic was not unanimous. Children displayed hunger bellies and babies died. Garbage piles were foraged in the hopes that someone might have left some small item of food.

On the day that things seemed, humanly-speaking, totally hopeless and a day when the porters of the city expected to be instructed by the sheriff of Franeker to unbolt the doors, a few young women, unmarried, approached him as he walked through the streets.

"Sir," one tall young lady spoke for the group, "Sir, we ask that you listen to an idea that we have conceived."

The sheriff, weary with hunger, was slightly impatient. Yet, having no alternative, he motioned that the women come closer. He then noted with amazement that they all carried bread—fresh loaves of bread. The smell, reaching his nostrils, almost made him delirious with desire for a bit of the yellowish crust. He almost missed the entire first sentence one of the young woman spoke, and had to literally force himself to turn his head away from the sustenance in their arms.

"...so we took counsel and took the last bit of meal we had hidden away to bake these loaves."

The sheriff nodded, as if he understood, but indeed, he did not. The girl continued.

"We thought, therefore, that if we stood on the ramparts, we could, from behind the shoulders of the soldiers standing guard there, throw the bread down..."

At this the sheriff drew his breath in sharply. Saliva rebelled in his mouth, and he swallowed visibly. The girl smiled slightly and continued.

"This act might convey to the enemy that we have plenty of victuals; so much, as a matter of fact, that we are able to share some of it. It would also give the impression that, no matter how long we were besieged, it would do no good. We have also heard whispers, Sir Sheriff, that the soldiers on the other side grow weary with staying here, and that they want to go home. This act would increase their impatience and add to their unrest."

The sheriff stood undecided. He had not known whether it would be that day or the next that he would advise the city's council to surrender.

"It is worthy of consideration," he said at length. "Wait here and I will speak with the others."

The girls waited for one hour, for two hours and for several more, all the time holding on to their precious loaves. Every now and then they heard loud voices from the chamber where the leaders of the city met. Eventually, however, the men emerged. Some looked sourly and angrily at the group of girls and others smiled. The sheriff came out last. He walked up to the girls.

"Your plan has been approved," he said, adding with a thin smile, "Go about your business then, and go with God."

The girls consequently climbed the ramparts and threw down their loaves over the edge of the wall rather nonchalantly. The soldiers had been instructed to remain quiet and to smile, as if they did not care that the girls were dropping precious bread on the enemy side. They soon saw, to their satisfaction, that several infantry men were sent over to inspect the bread—to determine whether or not it was real.

Within hours, the bread incident had spread around the besieging campsite and that same day, a number of enemy soldiers mutinied. Slowly but surely, the army that surrounded Franeker disappeared. God had saved the day, and he had used the wisdom of a few, simple but wise girls to do so.

Food for thought

1. What is your first reaction in a situation of crisis: panic or prayer? Why?

2. Do you ask for counsel and listen to what others say when you have a problem, or are you prone to rely on your own judgement? Why or why not?

31

Luke 10:30–36 *"A man was going down from Jerusalem to Jericho, and he fell among robbers, who stripped him and beat him and departed, leaving him half dead. Now by chance a priest was going down that road, and when he saw him he passed by on the other side. So likewise, a Levite, when he came to the place and saw him, passed by on the other side. But a Samaritan, as he journeyed, came to where he was, and when he saw him, he had compassion. He went to him and bound up his wounds, pouring on oil and wine. Then he set him on his own animal and brought him to an inn and took care of him. And the next day he took out two denarii and gave them to the innkeeper, saying, "Take care of him, and whatever more you spend, I will repay you when I come back." Which of these three, do you think, proved to be a neighbor to the man who fell among the robbers?"*

The objective Samaritan

n July 1951, on a small train bound for the Russian city of Zagorsk, from Moscow, a singular incident occurred. This incident was recorded by a writer named Frank Rounds, who was in Russia to document the communist way of life.

Zagorsk is the location of a fourteenth-century monastery, with the imposing name of Troitse-Sergievska, and a popular place for tourists to visit. July 1951 was no different. On one of the last days of that month, a very hot day, thousands of Moscow dwellers, wanting to leave the dusty metropolis behind them, boarded the train bound for Zagorsk. They were by no means all destined to visit the monastery. Most, as a matter of fact, would leave the train before the final destination, getting off at the many *dachas*, or small country cottages, lining the countryside along the railroad tracks.

Frank Rounds was among the crowd of city-dwellers leaving Moscow. He was headed for the monastery and had decided to take the Russian railroad instead of using the embassy car to which he had access. Arriving at the railway station around noon, he had difficulty getting inside the waiting train. The cars appeared to be bursting at the seams with people. They leaned out of the train windows, jam-packed the open doors and completely covered the platform. The air was humid, stale and unhealthy. It seemed that everyone was extremely anxious to get out of Moscow for the weekend.

Rounds eventually managed to get onto the train. Shoulder to shoulder in the aisle with several people, he half regretted going this route, but then reflected that he would get to know the Russians more intimately this way. No one spoke, but neither did anyone push anyone else unnecessarily. But all at once there was some commotion. Peasant women carrying baskets, children with toys and well-dressed people holding onto overnight cases, jostled him. It seemed that a drunk man, just a few paces away, had fallen over. Not only that, but he lay on the floor totally oblivious, unconscious and unaware that a host of people stood around him. He was dirty; his clothes were tattered, and his face wore several days' growth of whiskers.

Not too many minutes later, the crowd, as if one, moved to take back the room it had been forced to concede. They stepped on the man where he lay, stepped on his rags; his filth and his breath touched their legs. The man's face was bleeding, and his mouth foamed a little.

After a few stops, the space became more manageable. People got off, the air became a bit fresher and the drunk could lie in relative peace. He moaned a little, but was not given attention by any of the people just above him. All were intent on their own various destinations.

Frank Rounds now took out a book he had taken along to while away his time on the train. The book was called *Resurrection*. The author, who was Leo Tolstoy, was describing someone's thoughts as another train had pulled out of Moscow around 1900:

> It is terrible to see men deprived of the chief human attributes: love and sympathy for one another...people acknowledge as law what is not law, and do not acknowledge as law at all, the eternal, immutable law written by God in the hearts of men.

Frank Rounds, after reading a bit more, put his book down and wondered what Russians, especially his fellow passengers on the train, felt like when they read this passage. Rounds knew that Tolstoy's views were Christ-like, and that he had a burning message for humanity. And as he studied his fellow passengers, he roundly condemned their detached attitudes—their lack of love for a passenger down on his luck.

At Zagorsk, Rounds got off the train. The man was still lying on the floor.

Food for thought

1. What are your thoughts on Frank Rounds? The dirty, pitiable drunken wretch lay not only at the feet of fellow travellers, but also at his own feet. He himself had also stepped on the man. Who was the worse sinner, Frank or his fellow passengers? Or, is that question not fair? Why or why not?

2. We daily see people whom Jesus classifies as our neighbours. If we want to act in a Christ-like manner, then we must love them as ourselves. What would you have done if you had been Frank Rounds?

32

1 Corinthians 6:9–11 Or do you not know that the unrighteous will not inherit the kingdom of God? Do not be deceived: neither the sexually immoral, nor idolaters, nor adulterers, nor men who practice homosexuality, nor thieves, nor the greedy, nor drunkards, nor revilers, nor swindlers will inherit the kingdom of God. And such were some of you. But you were washed, you were sanctified, you were justified in the name of the Lord Jesus Christ and by the Spirit of our God.

The stuffed mouse

Charlemagne (A.D. 742–814), King of the Franks and Holy Roman Emperor, was the grandson of Charles Martel, the famed Hammer who defeated the invading Muslims in the Battle of Tours in A.D. 732. Many stories circulate about Charlemagne, and the following anecdote could be either truth or legend. Whether one or the other, there is an aura of wisdom about it from which we can learn.

There was in Charlemagne's realm a bishop who had the reputation of being a vain and greedy man—a man who sought worldly approval rather than God's approval. So horrendous was the bishop's reputation that word of his avarice reached the emperor's ears. Wishing to teach the bishop a lesson, Charlemagne called to himself a Jewish merchant. The merchant was well known for his travels and for the rare and wonderful things he often brought back with him from his trips to other countries.

"You have my permission," Charlemagne said to the merchant, "to go and deceive the bishop. Cheat him in whatever way you can and then come and tell me what exactly you have done."

The merchant thought long and hard, and eventually struck upon an idea. He caught an ordinary little grey mouse, stuffed it full of spices, painted it a garish color and then went with the dead creature to the bishop. Given an audience he drew out the animal, fat and painted and stuffed full of spices.

"This never-before-seen animal," he began, "is most precious and comes from the land of Judea."

The bishop, immediately craving this unique and strange animal from the Holy Land, offered the merchant three pounds of silver for the creature. The merchant yawned.

"A fine price you would indeed be getting for so precious an article!"

The bishop, now all the more eager, offered ten pounds of silver.

"I had rather throw this unusual animal into the sea than let any man have it at so cheap and shameful a price," responded the merchant indignantly.

Then the bishop, who was extremely wealthy but never gave to the poor, bargained for twenty pounds of silver. And the fat, "Judean," stuffed mouse, a seemingly incomparable treasure at this point, sat beady-eyed and mute on the bishop's table. The merchant hid a smile behind his hand as he stood up.

"Heaven forbid," he cried out, "that I should thus let the fruit of much labour and journeying go."

He began to wrap the dead mouse in costly silk and made as if to leave. Consumed by desire, the bishop finally offered fifty pounds of silver. So it was that the little corpse of the mouse was sold for fifty pounds of silver.

The merchant, taking the silver directly to Charlemagne, related the whole matter to him in detail.

Not long after, Charlemagne called together the chief leaders and bishops of his kingdom for a meeting. He discussed various matters with them, and after all business had been concluded, ordered a servant to put fifty pounds of silver on the table. Then he stood up and spoke.

"Fathers and guardians, bishops of the Church. It is so that as examples you ought to minister to the poor, or rather to Christ. You ought not to seek after vanities. But often I fear a number of you are contrary, vain-glorious and avaricious."

Many around the table fidgeted nervously, for there were a number who did not look after their congregations as they should. Charlemagne continued to speak, as he pointed to the heap of coins.

"Look at all this silver! Look at it shine and look at the quantity! Would you believe that one of you has given a merchant all this silver for a stuffed and painted mouse thinking it to be a unique treasure!"

The bishop, feeling horribly betrayed, guilty and afraid, threw himself at Charlemagne's feet and begged pardon for his sin. Charlemagne upbraided him for a length of time, lambasting him for his greed. At length, however, he forgave the man, who seemed truly sorry, permitting him to go, hopefully, a more generous and gracious bishop.

Food for thought

1. You might chuckle at the story and deride the vain bishop, but is it not so that we all too often purchase stuffed mice ourselves? We listen to merchants praise their goods, and then we buy things that are not necessary simply to satisfy hearts full of vanity and greed. Those things could be expensive clothes, cars, computer hardware or just some small trinkets of cheap and passing worth. Comment.

2. There is no human emperor who will call us to account around a table, but surely we should be in awe of the One who made us stewards of his kingdom and who will call us into account on judgement day. Who is that? How can we appear before him?

33

John 3:16–21 *For God so loved the world, that he gave his only Son, that who-ever believes in him should not perish but have eternal life. For God did not send his Son into the world to condemn the world, but in order that the world might be saved through him. Whoever believes in him is not condemned, but whoever does not believe is condemned already, because he has not believed in the name of the only Son of God. And this is the judgment: the light has come into the world, and people loved the darkness rather than the light because their works were evil. For everyone who does wicked things hates the light and does not come to the light, lest his works should be exposed. But whoever does what is true comes to the light, so that it may be clearly seen that his works have been carried out in God.*

A grave mistake

The pain began on Tuesday, April 18, 1881, just before midnight. Charles woke his wife, to tell her that he was dying, and she ran for his pills. Together with a servant, she also administered brandy. But he was unable to keep it down, and retched miserably. He slept a little but vomited throughout most of the next morning, his body heaving and shuddering in agony. "If I could but die," he said repeatedly, intent on present escape and not focused on the fact that he would shortly face the Creator of his heart, the Judge of his soul. He vomited again and blood spewed out, spilling red onto his white and venerable looking beard. "Oh, God," he cried, and again, "Oh, Lord God." His pain appeared to be excruciating and lasted until he lost consciousness about a half hour before he died. And then Charles Darwin was no more on the earth that he had with human clarity consigned to evolutionary origins.

Charles Darwin (1809–1882) was the youngest son of an English doctor—one who did not believe in God. Young Charles liked the outdoors. He revelled in collecting shells and bird eggs. Although his father wanted him to become a doctor, like himself and his father before him, Charles had no interest in following their footsteps. He dropped out of medical school, studied theology for a while, and then went on to become a naturalist.

In 1831, when Charles was twenty-two, he was hired as a naturalist aboard a ship called the HMS *Beagle* and left England for a five-year excursion around the world. During this trip, Darwin was particularly intrigued by the plants and animals on the Galapagos Islands, several hundred miles off the west coast of South America. His conclusions at the end of this trip are well known. He inferred that all species—the entire plant and animal kingdom—had resulted from environmental adaptations over millions of years. In other words, God had not created the world in six days, but the world was the product of millions of years of evolution. In 1859, Darwin published these conclusions in a book entitled, *On the Origin of Species*.

Darwin had expressed the wish to be buried in the churchyard of the village of Downe, some sixteen miles south of London, where he had lived and worked most of his married life. He wanted his grave to be under a great yew tree next to the graves of three of his children. But such was the mood of the day, that a fool without clothes could be held up as a king—that one who had openly flouted God could be hailed as a saint.

Free-thinking friends, wanting to honour the dead atheist, presented the Dean of Westminster with the request that Charles Darwin be buried within that church. Petitions went around and many influential government people signed, indicating that they thought Darwin's last resting place should be one of glory among other English patriots. And it was arranged.

The funeral was not attended by either Queen Victoria or William Gladstone, her Prime Minister. Neither had expressed an appreciation for evolution. But thousands of others did attend. Judges, Parliament members, the Lord Mayor of London, ambassadors, scientists and a great many people from the ordinary homes and hearths of London. Multitudes entered the abbey, all handing in their funeral tickets at the door. After these had all settled in their pews, the doors opened to those who had no tickets. At noon a choir entered singing, "I am the resurrection." The family, flanking the coffin, which was draped in black velvet and covered with white blossoms, followed. A specially composed hymn was sung after a Bible lesson. The words of the hymn came from Proverbs: "Blessed is the man that findeth wisdom, and getteth understanding."

It is not entirely strange to suppose that the devil occupied one of the pews of Westminster that day. He, for one, was well aware that Darwin had said, "If God had planted the knowledge of His existence in humans, all would possess it." He also knew Darwin had said that "the plain language of the New Testament seems to show that the men who do not believe, and this would include my father, brother and almost all my best friends, will be everlastingly punished. And this is a damnable doctrine." And the devil must have slapped his knees in mirth thinking about Darwin's public confession: "I am sorry to have to inform you that I do not believe in the Bible as a divine revelation, and therefore not in Jesus Christ as the Son of God."

In the end, Darwin's coffin was lowered underneath Newton's monument as the choir rendered another selection, "His body is buried in peace, but his name liveth evermore." People were awed at the solemnity of the moment and at length the mourners filed out leaving Charles Darwin's body beneath the cold cement of Westminster Abbey.

Food for thought

1. Does it matter how or where one is buried? Why or why not? Can you prove this from the Bible?

2. Darwin referred to *On the Origin of Species* as "my accursed book." In the year leading up to publication, he was rarely able to write for more than 20 minutes at a time without stomach pains, and he finished the proof on October 1, 1859, between fits of vomiting. Is it possible that God was showing compassion to Darwin by physically trying him at this time?

34

Psalm 91:1–6 *He who dwells in the shelter of the Most High will abide in the shadow of the Almighty. I will say to the Lord, "My refuge and my fortress, my God, in whom I trust." For he will deliver you from the snare of the fowler and from the deadly pestilence. He will cover you with his pinions, and under his wings you will find refuge; his faithfulness is a shield and buckler. You will not fear the terror of the night, nor the arrow that flies by day, nor the pestilence that stalks in darkness, nor the destruction that wastes at noonday.*

You will not be afraid of the terror by night

Pastor Bernardus Smytegelt served a congregation in Middelburg, Holland, during the late 1600s. One late evening during a particularly cold and windy November, someone knocked at the door of Pastor Smytegelt's parsonage. Upon opening the door, he found a man whom he did not know begging him to come to the bedside of his dying friend. Giving the pastor a crumpled paper with the address on it, the man did not wait but quickly disappeared into the darkness. Rev. Smytegelt did not worry about or mistrust the man's motives. Always ready to help people, he immediately donned his heavy coat, lighted a lantern and set out for the given address. The wind whistled and the streets were deserted. As he approached a bridge, suddenly two dark figures emerged out of the shadows of a docked vessel. The pastor, thinking they were sailors, greeted them cordially and passed on. Upon reaching the indicated address, he knocked at the door, only to find out moments later that no one there had requested his presence and that no one there was dying. Obviously there had been a mistake. Nonplussed, the pastor returned to his home.

Two years later, again during the month of November when cutting winter winds once more howled their wild songs about the streets of Middelburg, there was another knock at the door of Rev. Smytegelt's parsonage. Once more a stranger begged the minister to come to the bedside of a dying friend. Perhaps the minister recalled the time when he had gone on an unfruitful visit two years before—or perhaps he did not recall. After all, there were many sick calls. Whatever the case, Rev. Smytegelt again did not hesitate to put on his great coat and without qualms accompanied the stranger to a grand mansion in the best part of town. He was surprised to find that the mansion belonged to one of the city councillors—a councillor who had violently opposed a number of social measures that he had tried to implement.

A butler ushered the pastor upstairs to an ornate bedroom. In this bedroom, resting on a magnificent bed replete with canopy, was the councillor. The man had his face turned toward the wall and would not look at Rev. Smytegelt as he stood by the bed. But he immediately began to speak.

It was I who came to your door in the dead of night some two years ago. It was I who lied to you and said that someone needed you at his bedside. I merely used the story as a ruse to get you to come out so that I could murder you. Indeed, I had persuaded a friend to come with me. It was our plan to knock you down at the bridge and to throw your body over the bridge railing into the water. We knew your heavy coat would have dragged you down.

The man stopped and coughed. Then he turned his anguished face to look into Rev. Smytegelt's compassionate eyes.

"Why, friend," the pastor asked, "Why did you want to kill me?"

"Because," the councillor answered, "you spoke against some of the laws I wanted to enact. You saw through the selfishness that motivated me and the other councillors and you were not afraid to expose our sins. I hated you for that."

"Why then," the pastor continued to ask, "did you not carry out your murder?"

"I could not."

The councillor half-sat up in his bed, leaning against the cushions that supported his back.

"You could not?"

Rev. Smytegelt tried to understand.

"Were you sorry? Did you feel remorse at the last moment?"

"No."

The answer was short and terse, and the sick man was shaken by a paroxysm of coughing before he continued.

As you approached we were itching to revenge ourselves on you. We were eager to hurt you and drop your body into the black water below, but suddenly, even as we were moving toward you, there were two men with you. Two men—one on either side of you. They walked next to you as you crossed over the bridge and they carried swords—flaming swords.

Rev. Smytegelt smiled. "You were kept from a great wrong, my friend."

"I could not die without confessing...without speaking to you... It has confounded me these last two years, and now here I am about to die."

It is not clear how the story ends, but it is to be supposed that Rev. Smytegelt prayed with the man, and encouraged him to put his trust in the One who can forgive sins.

Food for thought

1. The amazing thing about this story is that Rev. Smytegelt had not been aware of danger, had not directly asked for protection, but God had protected him regardless. Do you suppose God has ever protected you without you being aware of it? Can you think of a time?

2. Read Psalm 91:1–6 again. Is this your comfort?

35

Ecclesiastes 12:6–7
Remember him
  before the silver cord is snapped,
  or the golden bowl is broken,
  or the pitcher is shattered at the fountain,
  or the wheel broken at the cistern,
  and the dust returns to the earth as it was,
  and the spirit returns to God who gave it.

Remember him

The majority of people walking through this life do not bother to remember God at all, let alone remember that their purpose in life is inextricably bound up with the fact that he exists. Because of this, many lives are purposeless, futile and a chasing after wind. Strangely enough, although most people do not want to remember God, they do want to be remembered themselves. From time to time, this wish to be remembered translates into behaviour—extraordinary behaviour.

In 1824 a small boy was born in France. He was named Jean-Francois. His father was a tight-rope walker and, as many small boys aspire to do, he wanted to follow in his father's footsteps—his father's harrowing footsteps. His father encouraged him in this. From the time that Jean-Francois first toddled, his father's hands steadied him. The small blond child practiced and practiced. Before he could say his ABCs, his tiny figure had already balanced earnestly across a rope. Jean-Francois didn't really mind the work. He understood and approved of the fact that many people admired and came to watch his father. They clapped enthusiastically whenever his father performed, even as his father clapped when he, Jean-Francois, performed for him. It became his goal to become as good a tight-rope walker as his father was. That day came. Then it became his goal to be a better tight-rope walker than his father. That day also came. And as his father's star grew dimmer, Jean-Francois' became brighter and brighter until the day arrived that he was known as the most daring and sensational high-wire man in Europe.

In spite of his fame, Jean-Francois Gravelet was dissatisfied. He wanted something more but was not too clear in his mind as to what that "something more" was. In 1851 he left Europe and joined a circus troupe in North America. The troupe happened to be playing near Niagara Falls and Jean-Francois, or Blondin as he was now known because of his blond hair, was much impressed with this natural wonder. An idea took shape in his mind. The mighty falls thundered, and the deep gorge challenged him. It challenged him for eight years, at which time he finally did what he had desired to do since he first looked at the swirling eddies below. He took a three-inch thick rope and stretched it out across the Niagara Gorge. On June 29, 1859, in front of a sizeable crowd, Blondin walked across the gorge on the wet and slippery rope. There were no slip-ups, and the crowds were delighted. They cheered and yelled as Blondin bowed and smiled against the backdrop of a black and frothing river. Niagara Falls thrived under the wave of tourism the blond tight-rope walker brought it. Blondin was wined and dined and spoken of in awe. Tens of thousands of people travelled from all over North America to see him risking his life as he walked across the gorge.

Blondin repeated his dangerous act again and again. Tired of performing it the same way, he occasionally dressed up as an ape.

At other times he would stop halfway across the rope and stand on his head, or he would take along a small chafing dish and cook himself an omelette while the river rushed on under his feet. The crowds loved it. His most sensational crossing took place when the Prince of Wales visited Niagara Falls one summer. Blondin was intent on impressing this member of the British royal house and advertised that he would carry a man across the falls on his back. He was surprised when no one replied to the advertisement and finally persuaded an ex-sailor to be his partner. Thousands bet on the event. Blondin carried the man easily. They were tied together with a short rope. If one felt the other falling, he was to throw himself in the opposite direction with the hope that the rope would hit the tight-rope. This plan never had to be put into action. Blondin flawlessly repeated the piggy-back ride a number of times. Needless to say, the Prince of Wales was impressed.

Blondin lived and died a little over a century ago. He is buried and, for the most part, forgotten. Although the tightrope appeared to sustain him during his life, his own silver cord would not hold and was severed in 1896, at which time his dust returned to the ground.

Food for thought

1. If you are really honest, what is it you want people to say and think about you? Why?

2. How can you incorporate the phrase John the Baptist uses about Christ, "He must increase, but I must decrease," into your own life?

36

John 14:27 Peace I leave with you; My peace I give to you. Not as the world gives do I give to you. Let not your hearts be troubled, neither let them be afraid.

The death train

Not too far from the Pyrenees, in the south of France, stands Château de la Hille, an old French castle. A medieval fortress, it is surrounded by a high stone wall. Remnants of a drawbridge lean in front and four towers square it off. The surrounding countryside is pristine. A brook trickles merrily, pine trees sway in the wind and birds warble. It seems an altogether idyllic setting for a knight errant and a beautiful damsel, and, as the fairy tales have it, a place to live happily ever after.

During the Second World War, the Swiss Red Cross somehow

obtained the rights to the premises of this building. They obtained it with the purpose of sheltering Jewish children. From 1941 on, Château de la Hille housed and fed approximately 100 homeless children. Some of the children were orphans and some were just lost due to the ravages of Hitler's madness—but all were in desperate need of care.

Rösli Näf, a Swiss Red Cross nurse directed the affairs at Château de la Hille. Unmarried, hard-working and dedicated to protecting those in her care, she was shocked on August 25, 1942, to find that the French police had surrounded the castle with some sixty armed officers. There was nothing she could do to prevent them from arresting the thirty-nine oldest Jewish children. These children were teenagers—seventeen and eighteen years old.

The children were taken directly from the château by bus to a concentration camp at Le Vernet. They all had names—names like Ruth, Adele, Margot, Edith, Frieda... Charles, Henri, Hans, Walter, Pierre... names that children today carry as well. And in spite of their age, an age which often feels it has an edge on wisdom, they were afraid. Many had lost parents in Germany when these had been shipped to Dachau and other death camps; many had lost brothers and sisters, uncles and aunts and grandparents; and, with a sinking feeling, many felt certain they were also going to disappear.

Camp Le Vernet was a way-station to the east. It was merely a stop between France and Germany or Poland. Every time it was filled to capacity, people were moved out by trains and not heard of again. The children were not one hundred percent sure of these things. At Château de la Hille, these were matters of which no one spoke. But as they got off the rickety, old bus that had transported them to the camp, they sensed death. They smelled it. Issued a small piece of cardboard with a number written on it, they were told to hang it around their necks. They avoided looking at one another and stood quietly. Separated into male and female groups, they were assigned to barracks.

Although life at Château de la Hille had not been easy, the children had eaten. Even if they had never been quite full, they had definitely not starved. Now, at Camp Le Vernet, they were forced to forage garbage bags for empty tin cans so that when the small rations of moldy, watery food were doled out they would have some semblance of an eating utensil. Water was available for only two hours each morning, and the entire camp population of approximately 1,000 people had to compete for a few water faucets. No mattresses covered the wooden bunks, bunks which were so crowded that during the night hours everyone was forced to sleep on their sides.

The children from Château de la Hille whispered among themselves after they had been at the camp for a few days. They realistically speculated, after hearing fellow inmates speak, that they would soon be sent to one of the camps in Poland. On the fifth day, rumours ran rampant that a train was on the way and a transport would be sent east shortly. That evening, when the guards told the children to be ready to leave the next morning, they knew all hope of returning to the Château was futile. They were as good as dead.

At six o'clock the following morning they were up. By 8 o'clock, the 300 people in their barracks, as well as people in front of the other barracks, were lined up and waiting. The camp's gate gaped wide. A train of cattle cars stood just off to the side of the gate, the doors of the cars black and open. One by one, as names were called out, people disappeared through the doors into the train. Endlessly they filed as the list went on and on. But when the list was finished and folded, and when the doors of the cattle cars had closed, thirty-nine children were left standing in front of their barracks. Ten minutes later the train, the death train, began its slow trek east. The children did not move and neither did any of them speak. They hardly understood what had happened. A French commander came and stood in front of the group.

"Wait for Rösli Näf," he said, "and she will take you back to your Red Cross Home today."

"Merci, monsieur," they replied.

It happened as the commander said. That same day they were checked out, and that same day they returned with Rösli to the Château de la Hille. Rösli, it seemed, and another Red Cross official, had taken it upon themselves to approach France's chief of security after the children had been taken captive. Arranging a meeting, they had threatened that all aid to French refugee children would be suspended if the Château children were not released. Although Rösli and her friend had not had the authority to carry out their threat, providentially their ploy had worked. The French chief of security had grudgingly agreed to release the Jewish children.

This is a true story, and we should applaud Rösli Näf and her friend for their perseverance in getting the children away from the death train. But the story ends there. We don't really know what happened to the children after this episode because the reprieve from death obtained for them by Rösli Näf was only a temporary reprieve. Death would one day come for all thirty-nine of the children, as indeed, it inevitably comes for all of us.

Food for thought

1. The fact is that we are all like these children. The earthly years, the years given to us by the Giver of all life, are our barracks. We live in them and the train, the train of death, pulls in sooner or later. Regardless of who we are—rich, poor, talented, beautiful, young or old—the train pulls in for us all, often without warning. The lists are read hourly, and the train, no respecter of time or persons, pulls out continually. How then should we live?

2. There is One greater than Rösli Näf. And that one is Jesus Christ. And he has given his children a reprieve that far surpasses the one she obtained for the children of Château de la Hille. What is this reprieve? Can you quote texts to prove this reprieve?

37

Proverbs 11:4 *Riches do not profit in the day of wrath, but righteousness delivers from death.*

A chapter in the life of Jemmy Wood

emmy Wood was born in 1756 in Gloucester, England, into a middle-class family. Jemmy's grandfather had established the Gloucester Bank in 1716, and this bank, although primitive in its first few decades, began to solidify as Jemmy's father took over. Later, as Jemmy became a young man and learned the ins and outs of bookkeeping, of borrowing and lending, of accounts payable and accounts receivable, the bank became even better established. As a matter of fact, when Jemmy was middle-aged, Wood's Bank, as it was familiarly known, employed two or three clerks and conducted an increasing amount of business with many local shops.

Jemmy Wood was thrifty to the point of stingy. This meant that although he made a great deal of money (he was considered in his later years to be one of the richest commoners in England), he spent next to nothing. His days were consumed as those of Dickens' Scrooge were consumed—in the bank located at the end of a common chandlery shop. (This shop was also owned by Jemmy and run by his clerks.) When Jemmy went home at night, he was alone. He was not married, and he never invited company over for dinner. He did attend church on Sunday but, as during the week, he did not seek out company but returned home alone. Even the walk after his Sunday dinner was a solitary constitutional.

Jemmy Wood employed a little boy as house servant. This boy cleaned, cooked and acted as a miniature butler. One Sunday, before leaving his home to attend church, Jemmy handed the child a chicken.

"Roast it," he commanded, "so that it might be ready for me to eat when I return from the service."

The boy nodded and saw his master out the front door. Then he proceeded to the kitchen to put the bird on the spit. It took an hour or two and then a savory smell began to permeate the kitchen and the other rooms. The boy, whose nose was being fed, felt his mouth water. He had never been overfed. He sighed, and his stomach growled. Almost without warning his hand ventured to touch the browning skin of the bird. He ran his index finger along the skin and then brought it to his mouth. Then after the juice of the fowl had further whetted his appetite, his hand stole back to the breast, and he tore off a small piece of meat. The morsel titillated his senses, and his stomach growled again. Chewing carefully to make the piece last, his eyes glazed over in ecstasy. Then hunger defied reason and morsel after delectable morsel found its way into his mouth. And even though he was well aware that his master's steps were very likely wending their way back to the house, that did not stop his hand from continuing to bring the tender bits of flaky flesh and succulent crust to his lips. In the end, his stomach no longer gnawing with hunger, he eyed the bones in a mildly surprised manner. The chicken had totally disappeared! The spit was empty!! And there was no visible dinner for Master Wood!

The boy, suddenly realizing the immensity of his crime, began to tremble. After he had wiped his greasy fingers on his pants, he fell to thinking where he could possibly hide. For surely his master would beat him, or perhaps he would turn him over to the magistrate. But it was neither the thought of a beating nor of the sternness of the magistrate that made him tremble as much as the thought of the old man's countenance. Backing out of the kitchen, it was almost as if Jemmy Wood's piercing, hawk-like eyes devoured him. There was, he knew within himself, really no point in hiding. He would be found out. And yet, his feet kept moving away from the kitchen into an adjoining room. There he opened a closet, intending to enter and expecting to shut the door behind himself. But on the shelf, within reach, he saw a bottle labeled "Poison." To his quaking mind and heart, poison was much to be preferred to Master Wood's anger. He unscrewed the top, closed his eyes, and gulped down the entire contents of the bottle.

Shortly afterwards, Jemmy Wood walked in through the front door. He put down the umbrella which he had taken along in case of inclement weather, hung up his coat on the coat rack, and appreciatively sniffed the aroma of fried chicken. Unconsciously he licked his lips. Some brandy and water would go exceedingly well with that chicken.

"Boy, I'm home!" he called, adding, "Set the table and be quick about it."

When there was no answer, nor any detectable clatter of noise from the kitchen, he went to investigate. Seeing the chicken bones on the table, he raised his eyebrows. Some moments later he found the child lying on the closet floor with an empty bottle in his hand. The lad was stone drunk. The bottle in his hand contained brandy—brandy which Jemmy Wood usually drank by himself out of a bottle he had marked "Poison" so that no servant would ever touch it.

It is not known what Jemmy Wood did with the child after he awoke from his drunken stupor. (The boy did live to tell the story.) Perhaps shocked that the child would so fear him that he would prefer poison over facing him, the master showed mercy. Or it could be that he put the child out in the street without pay. Or yet again, maybe the incident caused him to feel shame for his extreme stinginess and made him to dwell on the fact that he must give account to God before long of all his goods. The latter is not likely as, upon his death, Jemmy Wood left several wills of a conflicting character. These documents caused litigation providing fodder for lawyers and much courtroom action lasting years after he died.

Food for thought

1. This single chapter in the life of a long ago banker is rather shocking. William Hendriksen, in his commentary on Luke writes:

> Make me, O Lord, a child again,
> Obedient to Thy call,
> In self possessing nothing, and
> In Thee possessing all.

Are you or are you not the kind of person Willliam Hendriksen wrote about? Why?

2. What do you think Proverbs 30:8–9 means when it says:

> Remove far from me falsehood and lying; give me neither poverty nor riches; feed me with the food that is needful for me, lest I be full and deny you and say, "Who is the Lord?" or lest I be poor and steal and profane the name of my God.

38

John 6:53–56 *So Jesus said to them, "Truly, truly, I say to you, unless you eat the flesh of the Son of Man and drink His blood, you have no life in you. Whoever feeds on My flesh and drinks My blood has eternal life, and I will raise him up on the last day. For My flesh is true food, and My blood is true drink. Whoever feeds on My flesh and drinks My blood abides in Me, and I in him."*

Reflecting on blood

There is a building in Germany today known by the name of *Jüdisches Krankenhaus Berlin*, which translated reads Berlin Jewish Hospital. When in April 1945, the victorious Soviet troops succeeded in taking over a stretch of Berlin neighbourhood on the Iranische Strasse they found, much to their amazement, a hospital sheltering hundreds of Jewish people—doctors, nurses, patients, non-medical staff and others. A spokesman stepped forward, greeting the Russians.

"This is a Jewish hospital," he said, cautiously continuing with, "and we are Jews."

There were 800 Jews there on that particular day. In an upper room of the administration building of the hospital, reports had carefully been filed away documenting these last Jews of Berlin.

Behind barbed wire, in what had been until 1944 the hospital's pathology department, the Gestapo had maintained Berlin's last *Sammellager*, or holding camp, where Jews awaiting deportation were kept until their number was sufficiently large to fill a transport to a concentration camp.

Only 162 of the people who met the Russians in April 1945 in the Berlin Jewish Hospital were full Jews. The amazing truth was that during the intensive bombing of Berlin during the latter months of the war, the hospital had hardly been damaged. A few bricks were loose, windows had shattered and much of the hospital grounds had been turned into a vegetable garden and cow pasture. There was also barbed wire surrounding the pathology building, but aside from that the hospital looked more or less the same as it had prior to the war. The words *Krankenhaus der Jüdischen Gemeinde*, or Hospital of the Jewish Community, were still solidly carved into stone above the main gate.

When the Soviets came, the hospital continued to function, but there remained only a very small group of Jewish doctors and nurses. Many had been deported. Day after day they, as well as their patients, had lived in fear of being on a list of people assigned for Auschwitz or other concentration camps.

After confiscating the pathology department, the Gestapo, during the last years of the war, had also taken the top floor of the hospital, turning it into a police ward for "war criminals." In 1944, one such "war criminal" was a man in his mid-thirties by the name of Fildermann.

Fildermann's middle name was Israel. (All male Jews were required to carry the middle name of Israel, and all female Jewesses the name Sarah on pain of arrest and deportation.) His first name is not known. The son of a prominent Jewish leader in Romania, he had been living in Cannes, France. The Germans arrested him there and took him to Berlin. He was thoroughly interrogated and kept in solitary confinement. It was thought that he might know the whereabouts of his father, and he was suspected of being in contact with him. For this reason, Israel Fildermann was not subjected to the brutal torture other prisoners had to endure. The Gestapo hoped he would furnish them with information, and when he did not confess they decided to keep him in the Jewish Hospital's police ward. In that ward, Israel Fildermann was again kept in solitary confinement. But even though interrogations were continued, he did not talk. The Gestapo eventually lost interest in him and Fildermann was allowed a little more freedom. He walked the grounds, was able to communicate with the staff and was fed as much food as they could supply. It was an established fact, however, that soon Fildermann would be placed on a transport and sent to a concentration camp.

At this point, the young man was diagnosed by the Jewish doctors at the hospital as a diphtheria carrier who needed to stay in isolation. The Gestapo had a horror of diphtheria. As a matter of fact, the diphtheria quarantine ward was the only place where the German police never set foot. A blood sample was needed, however, to verify Fildermann's condition. Consequently, the blood of another patient, who was known to test positive for diphtheria, was substituted. As a result, Israel Fildermann spent the rest of the war as a police ward diphtheria patient and was one of the group of people who greeted the Russians in April 1945. He had literally been saved by someone else's blood.

![black bar]

Food for thought

1. The Bible tells us very clearly that it is appointed for all men to die. That whole happy, excited group of people who greeted the Russians, including Israel Fildermann, would die regardless of the sweetness of that moment they experienced at liberation. And seeing that it is now more than seventy years after the fact, there is a good chance that most of them have already died. The blood of Fildermann's fellow patient did save his physical life for a certain period of time. However, whether or not Fildermann, or any of the others, were saved spiritually by Jesus' blood from the eternal concentration camp of hell is veiled from our knowledge. Why would or would it not make a difference to you if you could find out how Fildermann spent the rest of his life?

2. There is no distinction between Jew and Gentile. The same Lord is Lord of all and bestows his riches upon all who call upon him. Which final destination are you bound for?

39

Micah 5:2 *But you, O Bethlehem Ephrathah, who are too little to be among the clans of Judah, from you shall come forth for me one who is to be ruler in Israel, whose coming forth is from of old, from ancient days.*

Luke 2:15 *When the angels went away from them into heaven, the shepherds said to one another, "Let us go over to Bethlehem and see this thing that has happened, which the Lord has made known to us."*

Let us go over to Bethlehem

Bethlehem has become a popular name over the centuries. Many people have given that town's peaceful name to their associations, societies and buildings. There is one connecting word, however, we don't often link to the distinctive appellation Bethlehem. That word is "bedlam." Strange as it may be, the word bedlam has its root in the word Bethlehem. Even though bedlam means "riotous noise" and its very pronunciation makes you think of insanity, the truth is that its origin lies in the name of that little town where Jesus was born. So what is the connection?

In 1247, a priory was founded in London, England, called St. Mary of Bethlehem. Three-hundred years later, in 1547, the priory was given to the mayor and corporation of London and incorporated as a royal foundation for lunatics. Shortened to Bethlam or Bedlam, the building became the London lunatic asylum—a house of detention for the insane—and the wild ravings of its inmates gave the word *bedlam* its present meaning. Bedlam indicates a scene of wild uproar and confusion, and a bedlamite is a lunatic.

Over the years, Bedlam has had a mixture of patients. There were near-naked zanies, religious fanatics and the severely depressed. Baker and Willis, the most famous "mad doctors" of the 1700s, used powerful drugs, vomits and purges to quiet their patients. They also used a technique called cupping (drawing blood from the body by means of a cupping glass), leeches and blisters applied to the legs. As well, they shackled patients in chains, put them in darkened rooms, gave them cold showers, sat them in rotating chairs, applied electric shock treatments and shouted in voices of intimidation. Regarding madness as a disease of the body, they thought it required physical treatment.

There is a striking story of a man named Joseph Periam who was taken to Bedlam by his sister and committed there by her. Within the horrors of the prison-like facility, he took pen in hand and wrote a letter to a pastor. Here is the letter he wrote:

Dear Sir:
I have read your sermon upon the new birth, and hope I shall always have a due sense of my dear Redeemer's goodness to me, who has so infinitely extended his mercy to me, which sense be pleased to confirm in me by your prayers, and may Almighty God bless and preserve you. May he prosper your ministerial function. I wish, Sir, I could have some explanatory notes upon the New Testament to enlighten the darkness of my understanding, to make me capable of becoming a good soldier of Jesus Christ; but above all, I should be glad to see you. I am, dear Sir, yours affectionately with my whole heart, Joseph Periam.

Upon receiving and reading the letter, Rev. George Whitefield, the pastor, was troubled. It did not sound to him like Joseph was mad, but the letter he received was clearly post-marked Bethlam Hospital. Together with a friend, a Mr. Seward, he visited Joseph and found him to be a likeable, albeit eager, young man, of sound body and mind. Indeed, Rev. Whitefield had a good conversation with him. Returning home from the hospital, he resolved to visit Joseph's family, and he did so.

Receiving him amiably, although cautiously, Joseph's Periam's sister invited the minister in and seated him comfortably in a drawing room. Placing herself opposite the preacher, she listened when Rev. Whitefield expressed concern regarding her brother.

"I have spoken with your brother and found him to be quite sane."

"Oh, no, sir, you are mistaken. He is mad, to be sure."

"What makes you say so, Miss Periam?"

"There are three reasons, sir."

She fidgeted with her apron and was obviously agitated.

"What are they?" Rev. Whitefield asked.

"Well," she spoke softly, "the first is that he would not eat as we all did. He fasted, sir, for near a fortnight."

"And the second reason?"

"Well," she continued, looking at the wall, "he prayed so much and so loudly as to be heard four stories high."

"And the third reason you think him mad?"

Now the young woman looked at the floor and blushed.

"He," she faltered, "he sold his clothes and gave the money away without any thought in his head. He gave them to the beggars in the street."

"Indeed," Rev. Whitefield replied.

After a considerable amount of persuasive talk, Rev. Whitefield was able to make the sister understand that her brother was well on his way to becoming a Christian. That he had, upon reading the Bible, come across the story of the young man whom our Lord had commanded to sell all and give to the poor; that he had taken this accounting in the literal sense, and out of love for Jesus Christ had sold his clothes and had given the money to the poor. Although doubtful of this truth because she was not a Christian herself, the sister listened and was sympathetic. Later Rev. White-field wrote to a friend.

> Had the good pleasure of being an instrument, under God, with Mr. Seward, of bringing a young man out of Bethlam, who was lately put in that place for being, as they term it, methodically mad. I had become acquainted with him by way of letter.

We might, at this point, think of someone else besides Joseph Periam. A person who emptied himself and took the form of a servant; a person who, although a King, chose to be born in the likeness of men. And being found in human form he humbled himself even further and became obedient unto death, even death on a cross. Taken to be born in Bethlehem by his earthly parents, it had been purposed before time began that he was to be laid in a manger in that place. Was he mad?

The symptoms Miss Periam noticed in her brother were all present in Jesus. He fasted forty days and forty nights. He offered up prayers and supplications, with loud cries and tears. And he willingly gave, not only his clothes, but his body to be put to death for the sake of those beggars whom he, before the foundation of the world, had chosen.

Food for thought

1. Perhaps he who was born in Bethlehem will return this year. How will he find you a fool for his sake on earth when he returns?

2. The shepherds left behind their sheep and made for Bethlehem. They did not delay, they covered considerable distance, and they felt compelled to tell others what had happened to them, risking ridicule and disbelief. How do you spend the Christmas season?

40

Hebrews 12:1–2 *Therefore, since we are surrounded by so great a cloud of witnesses, let us also lay aside every weight, and sin which clings so closely, and let us run with endurance the race that is set before us, looking to Jesus, the founder and perfecter of our faith, who for the joy that was set before him endured the cross, despising the shame, and is seated at the right hand of the throne of God.*

Fixing our gaze

One of the first Brigids who ever lived was a woman who was born in Ireland, and she is classified as one of that country's patron saints (Patrick and Columba being the other two). Duvach, Brigid's father, was a chieftain. Brotseach (another tongue-twister) was the name of her mother. It is said that probably both Duvach and his wife were converted to Christianity under the preaching of Patrick around the middle of the fifth century. Irish lore has it that little Brigid, by all accounts, was a merry child. She was loving, gentle and compassionate, to man as well as to beast. Early in her life, the maiden resolved not to marry but to dedicate herself to the work of God as a missionary. She began a convent and was joined by other women who also desired to teach, preach and perform works of kindness.

If women today would think and dwell on God's Word as constantly as the faithful Brigid is recorded to have done, it would, without doubt, be a boon to society. Consider this. Brigid never ate until she had eaten of God's Word. She performed charitable works among the sick and maimed. She considered no physical work beneath her dignity. She was constant in hospitality, and she always meditated on the Lord.

However, there are also many negative threads wound about Brigid, though perhaps Brigid herself is not to be blamed for this. A legend both during and after her life, she was dubbed *Scotorum Gloria* or "The Glory of the Irish" or "The Mary of Ireland." Roman Catholic people have elevated her to a position worthy of veneration. Anecdotes about her, facts mingled with fiction, both fascinating and silly, began to circulate after her death. A few far-fetched examples will suffice.

On one occasion, it was said, a woodcutter killed a fox on the outskirts of a forest. The fox, unbeknown to the woodcutter, was the king's pet. The king, enraged to learn that his little Reynard had been killed, ordered the woodcutter killed, and his wife and children sold into slavery. When the woodcutter's friends asked Brigid to intervene, she got into her chariot and drove to the palace. As she drove along, she called out to another fox. This fox was so delighted with her voice that he immediately ran to her, jumped into the chariot and fell asleep within the folds of her garment. Arriving at the palace, she beseeched the king for the woodcutter's life. The king answered that he would spare the man's life only if a fox equal in cunning and tricks could be found. So Brigid (as you have probably guessed) gave him the fox she had picked up on her way to the palace—a fox whose tricks and gambols rivalled those of the king's dead pet. After this, the story goes, the king released the woodcutter, as well as his wife and children.

Another tale relates that Brigid once visited the home of a great man to ask him to release one of his prisoners. The great man was not at home, but the servants received Brigid hospitably. While she waited, she noticed some harps hanging on the walls and asked the servants to play some melodies for her.

"We do not have the skill to play," the men replied, "and, alas, the bards have gone with our master."

One of Brigid's companions then spoke.

"Bless our fingers, good mother," he said, "and we will play for you."

Brigid touched their fingers with her own and prayed. Consequently, when the young men took down the harps, they were able to play with such sweetness and power that it enthralled all who listened. The master returned home during this concert and wondered who was playing his harps. He was so amazed that unskilled men could make such music that he (you guessed it again), was put in the right frame of mind to release the captive from his jail.

One last little miracle! It is said that whenever Brigid was in a food shortage dilemma (caused by travellers visiting without notice when milk supplies were low), she spoke to her cows. These cows, endowed with the same generous nature as their mistress, freely yielded another milking at her request.

Fictional stories, such as these, led to the Roman Catholic Church naming February 1 as the day of commemoration for Brigid's death. A feast is held for her on that day each year. Many Catholics contend that Brigid holds second place among women in the kingdom of God, with Mary, the mother of Jesus, holding the first. Brigid's shrine is often visited by pilgrims. The number of churches dedicated to her are innumerable. Countless families choose her as their protectress. Hosts of men swear by her. She is commemorated in the divine office in many churches. St. Brogan's hymn reads:

There are two virgins in heaven
Who will not give me a forgetful protection,
Mary and St. Brigid,
Under the protection of both we remain.

Brigid perhaps, had no inkling of the Grimm-like fairy tales that sprang up after her death. We don't really know. But there it is— idolatry with a capital "I."

Food for thought

1. "I must grow less," said John the Baptist, "and he must grow more." Roman Catholics may have their pockets full of saints, but we cannot be too smug about our Protestant pockets. We might not bow the knee to Brigid or other saints, but we do well to remember that we might bow to other things and people. Think of pride in self and in denomination. How can this lead to idol worship? On whom or what do you fix your gaze?

2. It does no harm to reflect on the positive aspects of Brigid's life. Let us just enumerate: she never ate until she had eaten of God's Word. She performed charitable works among the sick and maimed. She considered no physical work beneath her. She was fervent in hospitality, and she constantly meditated on the Lord. What do you do and why do you do it?

41

Proverbs 13:22 *A good man leaves an inheritance to his children's children.*

Testaments—Old and New

Wills are interesting to read. They tell you a lot about what a person deemed important and what he or she deemed unimportant. Some people write their will with a twist of humour and some with a desire to do some good with their money after their death. Two men who penned wills in interesting and unusual manners were William Glanville the Younger and John Knill.

William Glanville the Younger was a man who wrote out an unusual clause in his will—a will which he dictated in 1717. He directed that two pounds each should be given annually to five poor boys in his home parish of Wotton, which lies near Surrey, England. They could not be just any five poor boys, however. In order to qualify for the money, these boys had to fulfil certain requirements on the anniversary of Glanville's death.

The requirements stipulated by William Glanville the Younger for his beneficiaries were as follows. Firstly, these boys must be willing to travel to the cemetery. Secondly, once there, they must put both hands on his tombstone and recite by heart The Lord's Prayer, the Apostles' Creed and the Ten Commandments. Seeing that Glanville's death fell on the second of February, it is doubtful that any children would enjoy such recitations. But reciting was not all they had to do. Once they had satisfactorily intoned the memory work, they also had to read 1 Corinthians 15, which speaks of the resurrection and is part of the Anglican burial service. Hopefully the young lads were supplied with gloves of some sort, because after Scripture reading, they were expected to do one more thing—write out two verses of this chapter in a legible hand.

If Glanville had simply been concerned about giving the boys a lasting gift of worthwhile memory work, prodded on by a monetary reward, he need not have made graveside attendance a must. One can only speculate as to why he stipulated that the boys must place their hands on his tombstone. Perhaps he put stock in prayers for the dead; perhaps he feared an unreal purgatory; or perhaps he wanted to be remembered for something strange.

John Knill, our second writer of a unique testament, was the mayor of the Cornish fishing port of St. Ives. Not waiting until he died to be remembered, he began constructing a steeple—a forty-five foot triangular pyramid he named Knill's Steeple. This was, he told the people of St. Ives, to be a seamark for the shipping industry, which he wanted to build up, as well as his own tomb. While constructing this edifice, he also began to devise an elaborate graveside ritual to be begun upon his death. However his plan, did not quite work out the way he had envisioned. John Knill died, not in St. Ives, but in London in the year 1811. He was buried, not under Knill's Steeple, but near London at St. Andrews Cemetery.

Nevertheless, in spite of the fact that Knill was not buried at Knill's Steeple, "Knillian Games" were instituted and held every

July 25 in the city of St. Ives. Ten small girls, under the age of ten and daughters of local fishermen, are required to dance around Knill's Steeple for fifteen minutes after which they have to sing the "Old Hundredth" Psalm. Having done that, they each receive ten shillings. The fiddler who plays for the dancing girls is awarded one pound and two poor widows, older than sixty-four, who have chaperoned the girls to see that the ceremony is carried out properly and in good order, each receive two pounds. The generosity of the benefits for the local people continues. The head of the family of the most legitimate children of St. Ives, provided he has never been on welfare and is over the age of sixty, receives five pounds. As well, the "most worthy girl" who has married within seven months before the "Knillian Games" also receives five pounds, as does the best packer of pilchards or other fish.

After these "Knillian" ceremonies, the trustees of the Knillian Fund enjoy a free Knillian dinner. The Knillian Games are popular with tourists and are presently held every five years.

Food for thought

1. There is a website called Eulogy International on which you can shop for the best deals in burials. You can also get prepaid funeral planning or help on the Internet in writing your obituaries. Comment.

2. There is a eulogy written by Jesus himself, and his words ring with promise: "His master said to him, 'Well done, good and faithful servant. You have been faithful over a little; I will set you over much. Enter into the joy of your master'" (Matthew 25:21). Who is this obituary written for? Why or why not are you one of the recipients?

42

Ezekiel 3:18–21 *If I say to the wicked, "You shall surely die," and you give him no warning, nor speak to warn the wicked from his wicked way, in order to save his life, that wicked person shall die for his iniquity, but his blood I will require at your hand. But if you warn the wicked, and he does not turn from his wickedness, or from his wicked way, he shall die in his iniquity, but you will have delivered your soul. Again, if a righteous person turns from his righteousness and commits injustice, and I lay a stumbling block before him, he shall die. Because you have not warned him, he shall die for his sin, and his righteous deeds that he has done shall not be remembered; but his blood I will require at your hand. But if you warn the righteous person not to sin, and he does not sin, he shall surely live, because he took warning, and you will have delivered your soul.*

Helping others to laugh last

Guest speaker Michael Corin, host of TV and radio programs, gave a moving presentation at a graduation ceremony in packed auditorium at Redeemer University in Ancaster, Ontario. He recounted that when he walked the streets of nearby Hamilton he would occasionally be asked for handouts by the down-and-outers of that city. Once while passing some dumpsters he noticed that the garbage bags in one of them were moving. Soon, a man climbed out from between the bags—a man who had obviously made that place of refuse a place of refuge for the night. The man, who reeked of sour and decomposing things, made his way over to Michael Corin asking for money. Corin shook his head but offered to take the man out for a meal. The man accepted.

People stared at this pair walking through the streets. There was Michael Corin in his suit, dressed neatly; and there, closely trailing him, was a man in tatters. His pants were so ripped that his private parts were almost showing. He was altogether unlovely.

Their arrival at the restaurant caused a lot of heads to turn and a lot of noses to twitch. The tramp carried the smell of something akin to raunchy Limburger cheese overwhelming the smell of sweet cooking. It would have been funny had it not been so sad. Corin took the man to the smorgasbord section, filled a plate with food and walked over to the counter to pay. The girl at the checkout was obviously nonplussed and stared from the ragged man to Corin and back to the man again. The obscene smell palpably exuding from one of them made her ask a question.

"Are you together?"

She directly addressed Michael Corin, expecting him to deny any relationship with such a disgusting companion.

Michael Corin then related to the graduating class and to their families, teachers, friends and relatives, how very moved he had been within the very pit of his being by this question. It took him a moment to formulate a reply because, as he said, he rejoiced with great rejoicing at being able to answer positively.

"Yes, we are," he said, adding, "Thank God, we are."

You may not know this about me [he told the audience] because I look fairly respectable up here, without that mortar board of a hat, but if my thoughts and desires for only one hour of this day would be posted behind me, you would all be horrified by the depth of the totally black background confronting you.

He was quiet for a moment and thoughtfully chewed his lip as he continued.

For a split second as I stood there by the cash register with that poor stinking soul, it was as if I stood next to myself.

And for a split second I felt as if I'd been thrown into eternity. Clad in filthy rags I stood in front of the throne of almighty God. Vileness dripped off me and worthlessness encompassed me. And God's voice rang out.

"Are you together?" He asked the one standing next to me.

And the one who stood next to me answered clearly.

"Yes, we are," he said, "Yes, we are together."

Food for thought

1. If the graduating class remembers and takes to heart the theme of Corin's speech—awareness of sin, repentance and a life of thankfulness—and puts it into practice, what kind of lives do you think they will live?

2. Did you know that more than six billion people live on this earth? A population whose current growth rate is about 1.7 percent per year—six billion souls who all stem from Adam and who all have inherited Adam's sin. The truth is that as long as a sinner is alive, there is hope. Why do you think this brief account is titled, "Helping others to laugh last"? How are you willing to be used by God to help others to laugh last?

43

Mark 12:41–44 *And he sat down opposite the treasury, and watched the people putting money into the offering box. Many rich people put in large sums. And a poor widow came, and put in two small copper coins, which make a penny. And he called his disciples to him, and said to them, "Truly, I say to you, this poor widow has put in more than all those who are contributing to the offering box. For they all contributed out of their abundance; but she out of her poverty has put in everything she had, all she had to live on."*

Giving

N o matter how rich, no matter how poor, we all have some things we prize. We all regard some things in our possession as sweet—as wholly ours. Generally speaking, giving is related to "being able" to give. That is to say, when we put money in the Sunday collection plate, we are usually aware that our bank account is stable, the paycheque is forthcoming and the freezer is full.

Miss X, whose name is not known, lived during the 1800s. She was a needle women, a seamstress. It was not a lucrative occupation, earning an average of some three shillings a week. It kept hunger at bay but did not permit her to revel in linen sheets, goose-down pillows or silk dresses. No, Miss X was neither materially wealthy nor healthy, but quite frail and often succumbed to illness. Nevertheless, Miss X managed to live in the city of Bristol, England, with cheerfulness of heart and generosity of character. You have, no doubt, guessed her final citizenship. It was a heavenly one, for Miss X was a practicing Christian.

There are those people who are shy about being Christians. They never speak of the tremendous riches laid up for them in heaven.

> I have no notion of a timid, disingenuous profession of Christ. Such...are like a rat playing at hide-and-seek behind a wainscot, who puts his head through a hole to see if the coast is clear and ventures out if nobody is in the way, but slinks back again if danger appears. We cannot be honest to Christ except we are bold for him. He is either worth all we can lose for him or he is worth nothing.

Perhaps Miss X had heard Charles Spurgeon, who penned the above words. In any case, she lived her Christianity boldly. Her neighbours were well acquainted with the fact that she knew and loved her Saviour with all her heart. She attended church regularly, sang as she worked and did not complain of her circumstances.

Miss X did not have the benefit of a Christian home. Her brother and two sisters scorned her convictions and made fun of her. Her father was a drunkard. When he died, a small legacy of less than £500 came to her. He died bankrupt, and although the creditors had no legal claim on the four children for the money he owed, Miss X pondered the matter of her father's debt. With a certain amount of generosity, her brother and sisters, who had also received a legacy, paid one quarter of the amount their father owed. Miss X paid the remaining three quarters. The brother and sisters also gave £50 to their widowed mother. Miss X felt constrained to give £100. Her legacy, at this point, had shrunk considerably. And yet she had not done with giving. She took another £100 and donated it to a Christian orphanage.

The founder of the orphanage, before accepting this money, spoke with Miss X. He was afraid she might be giving in haste or without the right motive. But she, sitting in a chair in front of his desk, was not hesitant.

"The Lord Jesus," she said, "has given his last drop of blood for me, and should I not give him this £100?"

Miss X's friends and neighbours knew little of her giving so large a sum of money. She was not given to speaking of what she had done. But her manner of giving was an example of giving reminiscent of that woman of whom Jesus said, "...she out of her poverty has put in everything she had, all she had to live on."

After Miss X died, it came to light that she had often given away what little food and clothing she had to those poorer than herself. The love of Christ had completely enveloped her. Mercy had become second nature. Although the legacy was gone long before she died, she was never in want. God provided for her, even as she had so liberally given of all she had.

Food for thought

1. How is it possible for a person to be smug about giving? Is it important to do deeds of charity in secret? Why or why not? Should or should it not hurt to give? Should our giving exceed our earning?

2. Charles Spurgeon said:

> If we suck our consolation from the breasts of the world, we prove ourselves to be its homeborn children. Does the world satisfy thee? Then thou hast thy reward and thy portion in this life; make much of it, for thou shalt know no other joy.

With the story of the needle woman in mind, comment on this quote.

44

Proverbs 13:25 *The righteous has enough to satisfy his appetite, but the belly of the wicked suffers want.*

Poor Fletcher!

I n 1849, Horace Fletcher was born in Lawrence, Massachusetts. Probably very few people, if any, have ever heard of Horace Fletcher. Yet his name was coined into the word "fletcherizing"—a word generally speaking, we don't use much anymore.

So what exactly did Horace Fletcher do? And how important is it for us to be aware of what fletcherizing means?

As he grew up, Horace Fletcher proved to be an enterprising young man. Eager to see what life was about outside Massachusetts, he left for Japan on a whaling ship at the tender age of sixteen. Although he later returned to America and attended school at

Andover and Dartmouth, he had tasted Japan and liked the flavour. He went back and lived there for another six years, returning to America as an importer of Japanese art, toys and novelties. The business was so lucrative that, by the time he was forty, Horace Fletcher was a very wealthy man.

Not only a wealthy man, Fletcher was also a very versatile person. Claiming to have some thirty-eight occupations, he became the enthusiastic director of an opera company, was a reasonable amateur painter, a good athlete and president of the New Orleans Philharmonic. A very peace-loving, friendly man, Fletcher was nicknamed "Buddha" by those who knew him. Unruffled and serene, he had a sociable nature and entertained lavishly. He continued travelling the world, eventually settling down in a thirteenth-century palace in Venice.

In Venice, he enjoyed life to the full, becoming rather dignified around the waist. Standing only five-foot seven-inches high, he weighed 217 pounds. He was not upset by this fact until he applied for life insurance and was turned down because of his obesity. Forty-four years old at the time, he was quite mortified. Even as he had thrown his enthusiasm into other ventures, he now became tremendously interested in the health of body and mind.

After thinking on the matter a great deal, Fletcher proposed that ill health was caused by fear. Take away fear, he theorized, and you will eliminate disease. Positive thinking, he went on, will produce miracle cures of illnesses ranging from gout to insanity.

Fletcher was unable, however, not even with the most positive of thoughts, to lose those extra, irritating pounds. So he added new qualifications onto his theory. Pain, worry and fear, he fantasized, are caused by indigestion. And indigestion, Fletcher said, is probably caused by the fact that people do not chew their food properly. Because saliva is needed to mix food in the mouth, he concluded that thorough chewing was a necessity, with—a minimum of 100 chews a minute. Fletcher sat down, thought and then wrote 7 nutritional rules:

1. Never eat except when "good and hungry."
2. Never eat when badly worried or angry.
3. Eat only what really tastes good to you.

4. Exhaust all of the good taste from all food. Don't swallow any food until first it is like a pulp in your mouth and has been fully tasted. When this is so, the food will swallow itself.
5. Leave a little bit of the appetite as a "nest egg" for the next meal.
6. Eat always somewhat less than what you can; but eat what you do a little more, and so get far better results in the way of both pleasure and nutrition. It isn't how much you eat that does you good, it is how you eat and what you eat.
7. If you have only five minutes in which to eat, and do not expect to have another chance for a long time, don't hurry. A small amount of food thoroughly masticated is better than much more which is swallowed unmasticated.

Fletcher actually had a number of good points. He followed his own rules religiously and found that with less and simpler food, he was quite satisfied. Not surprisingly, his weight dropped considerably. He easily got by on some 1,600 calories, one third of the number recommended by the doctors at that time. He published his personal results, and his regimen of eating caught on. Fletcher's physique improved dramatically. He began volunteering for feats of strength, and newspaper reporters delighted in reporting how the fifty-year-old Fletcher outclassed younger competitors in races and in weightlifting. In July 1899, Fletcher took part in a 100 mile bicycle race though the French countryside. When he won, not even a bit winded, the public cheered. Later, at age fifty-eight he visited Yale and lifted 300 pounds 350 times in succession using only his calf muscles. They cheered again.

The enamoured public began to emulate Fletcher's chewing example, and the word "fletcherizing" was born. For a time, Edwardian London hosted "munching parties." At such gatherings, the master of ceremonies would employ a stopwatch to see how long it took each guest to chew a mouthful of food.

Fletcher was, by this time, known as the "chew-chew" man and his quotes, lifestyle and theories became exceedingly popular. Among some of his more famous fletcherizing adherents were Thomas Edison, John D. Rockefeller and Upton Sinclair. It was estimated that some 200,000 American families fletcherized in the first decade of the twentieth century.

Fletcher philosophized more and more as he grew older, and he became convinced that doctors would not be needed if the world would only chew properly. If the world would only realize the monumental benefits of fletcherizing, he postulated, the results would be nothing short of amazing. In his opinion the result of perfect chewing would be no slums, no degeneracy and no criminals. In a single generation, Fletcher believed, humankind's entire list of social problems would be solved.

During the First World War, Fletcher was sent to Belgium by President Hoover, as a food economist with the Commission for Relief. History does not record whether Fletcher's methods triumphed in Belgium. No experiments in mastication are documented in Europe. At the end of war, Fletcher contracted bronchitis, dying at the relatively young age of sixty-nine.

Food for thought

1. Fletcher is largely forgotten today. Living in a fast-paced, fast-food society, we can certainly learn from the list of suggestions Fletcher published. Our society has a lot of sedentary, overweight individuals who spend very little time either chewing or contemplating the blessings of a full plate of food. Meals with family, as well as conversation and a relaxed, unhurried atmosphere, are a great help to digestion. Topped off by devotions—Bible reading and prayer—they become indispensable to good health. Such healthful family times go a long way toward stemming delinquency, loneliness and other social issues. Comment.

2. Although Fletcher helped scientists rethink the standards for the minimum daily requirements for protein, he himself did not feed on the daily requirement for a healthy soul. What are the daily requirements for a healthy soul?

45

Luke 12:16–21 *And he told them a parable, saying, "The land of a rich man brought forth plentifully," and he thought to himself, "What shall I do, for I have nowhere to store my crops?"And he said, "I will do this: I will tear down my barns and build larger ones, and there I will store all my grain and my goods. And I will say to my soul, Soul, you have ample goods laid up for many years; relax, eat, drink, be merry."But God said to him, "Fool! This night your soul is required of you, and the things you have prepared, whose will they be?"So is the one who lays up treasure for himself, and is not rich toward God.*

Hoarding is idolatry

Webster's dictionary defines hoarding as accumulating money, food or the like, in a hidden or carefully guarded place for preservation or future use. So, if your mother cans vegetables and puts them in the cool cellar, is she hoarding? And how is hoarding idolatry—worship of something besides God?

There was a man who lived in France around 1762. It is recorded that he was wealthy, but no one really knew how wealthy, nor did they know where he kept the money that he earned. By some strange coincidence this man was a farmer—a farmer like the man recorded in Luke 12:16–21—the one who built barns and mocked the future. Foscue, for that was the French farmer's name, liked to gloat about all the money he had saved.

Foscue had built a vault underneath his farmhouse, a vault about which no one, except he himself, knew. Every now and then, Foscue would climb down into this vault by means of a ladder. One day as he climbed down into his vault, desirous of feeling accumulated coins slide through his fingers, the secret trap door slammed shut above his head, and he was locked into his hidden vault—alone with his money and his candle. His servants and, at length, the entire village, searched for him. They dragged the pool on his property, combed the woods and offered rewards from Foscue's own resources for the recovery of his being. But no one found him. He had no heir and the property he had taken such care to build up was sold, as was his house and barn. The new owner, after a period of time had elapsed, hired a number of workmen to make some alterations to the cellar. It was at this time that Foscue's body was discovered. It was found to be sitting upright between earthly treasures—treasures which glittered and shone—treasures for which he had served the devil. Beside the dead man lay a candle holder. It held no candle. In a last desperate attempt to stay alive, Foscue had eaten the candle, as well as gnawing the flesh on both of his arms.

It is a wonderful thing to have enough to eat, to have a roof over one's head and to have decent clothes to wear. This is a gift from God.

The preacher stresses this in Ecclesiastes 5:19 when he says: "Moreover, when God gives any man wealth and possessions, and enables him to enjoy them, to accept his lot and be happy in his work—this is a gift of God." Sometimes, however, this gift becomes entangled with self-deception, with greed and with no thought of the heavenly wealth God has prepared for all those who love him.

Governments and citizens alike are often overly concerned with material economy, with a common cents market of stocks, bonds and banks. They are usually not concerned enough with spiritual economy, a treasury-in-heaven market, a market of love, joy and peace.

Food for thought

1. We don't need two cars in our garage to qualify for a wealthy certificate; we don't need a swimming pool in our backyard to graduate from prosperous school; and neither do we need a millionaire's bank account in order to reach a moneyed status. How much does a person need in order to qualify as a miser?

2. Why is hoarding idolatry?

46

1 **Corinthians 13:8–13** *Love never ends. As for prophecies, they will pass away; as for tongues, they will cease; as for knowledge, it will pass away. For we know in part and we prophecy in part, but when the perfect comes, the partial will pass away. When I was a child, I spoke like a child, I thought like a child, I reasoned like a child. When I became a man, I gave up childish ways. For now we see in a mirror dimly, but then face to face. Now I know in part; then I shall know fully, even as I have been fully known. So now faith, hope, and love abide, these three; but the greatest of these is love.*

Yeddie's union

In the 1800s there lived a mentally challenged boy in the highlands of Scotland. His name was Yeddie, and he was a peaceable young man-child who, although dull of wits, would not harm anything or anyone. Yeddie lived with his grandmother in a small, poor cottage and spent his days walking the roads around the village where they lived. His ability to relate and speak with other people was severely limited, but he could often be heard whispering to himself. Neighbours gave him odd jobs, simple tasks which he performed with glee. They all tolerated him with affection and considered him as much a part of the landscape as the church steeple. He belonged.

Yeddie loved church and sat quietly during services, drinking in what words and doctrine he could understand. God was pleased to elect this rather slow, in the eyes of the world, child. Yeddie's child-like faith was endearing and many people remarked on it.

Sometimes boys, as boys will, would taunt the lad for mumbling to himself as he loped about the countryside.

"What ghost or goblin are you talking to now, Yeddie?" they yelled.

Unperturbed, he always answered back.

"Neither the one nor tither," he called out, in the Scottish dialect, smiling broadly as he spoke, "I was just having a few words with him that neither yousel' nor I can see, and yet with him that sees us all."

There came a day when Yeddie presented himself at the parsonage asking to see the minister. The servant girl who opened the door had a kind heart. She pitied the hulking figure of the shy fellow on the stoop.

"Come on in, Yeddie. Wait in the hall, mind, while I go and see if the minister can see you."

There he stood in the hall in his hob-nailed shoes and in his homespun shirt, looking at the floor. The door of the study at the end of the hall opened and the servant girl returned.

"The minister will see you, Yeddie. Mind your manners in there."

Yeddie smiled at the girl who smiled back. Then he tip-toed down the carpeted hall and entered the study. He closed the door behind him and bowed awkwardly before the pastor whom he greatly respected.

"What can I do for you, Yeddie?"

The minister spoke kindly.

"Oh, please sir, let poor Yeddie eat supper tomorrow with the Lord Jesus."

It was to be communion that Sunday. The area in which Yeddie lived was sparsely populated and not only Yeddie's church, but several other churches in the surrounding region were to participate in the communion as well. It would be an outside service, and many tables and benches had already been put up in the common. The minister thoughtfully stared out his window and did not reply. This greatly agitated the boy, and he begged again from the bottom of his heart.

"Oh, sir, if ye but kenned how I love him, ye wud let me go where he's to sit at table!"

The pastor looked at the pleading face of the man-child in front of him and thought of all those who would partake without the passion of this soul. Yeddie's hands were clasped together as if in prayer.

"Yes, Yeddie," he said, "you may sit at the table."

The boy laughed in joy, turned and ran out the door, not bothering to shut it behind him. He raced down the hall, his hob-nailed shoes no longer tip-toeing but making a great deal of racket. He was out the front door and down the road before the servant girl had a chance to let him out properly. She stood at the front door, which he had also left wide open, shaking her head but grinning.

The next day, along with everyone else in the district, Yeddie sat at the table of the Lord. As the service proceeded, he wept and whispered to himself. Those who sat next to him heard him say several times, "But I dinna see him."

After Yeddie partook of the bread and wine, however, he suddenly looked up at the minister, nodding and smiling with great joy. Then he covered his face with his hands and bent over, burying it between his knees. And that was the posture he kept until everyone had left and gone home.

Yeddie walked away from the table by himself. A group of boys, as was often the case, trailed him. But he turned from them, rebuking them.

"Ah, lads," he said, "dinna bid Yeddie talk today. He's seen the face of the Lord Jesus. He got a smile frae his eye and a word frae his tongue; and he's afraid to speak lest he lose the memory, for it's a bad memory Yeddie has. Ah, lads! I ha' seen him this day that I never seed before. I ha' seen yon lovely Man!"

Yeddie turned and the boys left, confused by his speech. And Yeddie, eventually reached the small cottage where his grand-mother had supper waiting for him—porridge and treacle. But Yeddie dared not speak much to his grandmother either, although he loved her exceedingly, lest he lose as he said, "the bonny face." He could not be cajoled into taking even one bite of the porridge in spite of the fact that he usually had what his grandmother termed as a "a fearful appetite."

"Nae meat for me, granny! I ha' had a feast just now. I supped with the Lord Jesus, and now I must go up to the loft and sleep wi' him."

Patting his grandmother's cheek, Yeddie climbed up a ladder to his loft to lay down on his pallet of straw so he might think on his lovely Man.

The grandmother, left below, heard Yeddie talking as she cleared away the uneaten plate of porridge.

"Ah, Lord," she heard her grandson say, "it's just poor me that has been sae long seeking ye and now we'll bide thegither and never part more!"

The grandmother shook her head. She stood undecided about whether to bid him come down again, but then thought it best to leave him to go to sleep.

"Oh, aye," she heard him call out a bit later, "but this is a bonny loft, all gold and precious stones! The hall o' the castle is a poor place compared to my loft this bonny night!"

She listened at the foot of the ladder, perplexed by the words, but Yeddie's voice grew softer and softer until it stopped altogether. To a neighbour who came by for a cup of tea, she related Yeddie's words, and the two of them wondered at God's ways.

The next morning Yeddie's grandmother rose early, poked the fire into flame and brought water up from a spring. Then she made porridge. Porridge was the staple for most of the meals.

"Yeddie! Time to rise, lad!"

She called normally at first, as she did most mornings, but when he did not answer, she let her lungs expand.

"Yeddie! Porridge is getting cold, boy! Get up!"

Again there was no reply. Carefully, after thinking for a while, she put a foot on the first rung of the rickety ladder, something she had not done for the last few years. Step by step, she ascended and at the top, slowly hoisted her tiny, old body onto the garret floor. Yeddie was sitting in front of a three-legged stool, the only piece of furniture in the garret besides the bed. He was half-sitting, half-kneeling. His eyes were closed. She could not understand it. He was dead.

But the truth was that Yeddie, who had seen through a mirror dimly, now saw face to face; the truth was that the child-boy who had known only in part, now understood fully.

Food for thought

1. Is piety knowledge? Is it true that those who have greater knowledge have greater piety? To whom belongs the kingdom of God?

2. Calvin said, "Not only does Christ cleave to us by an invisible bond of fellowship, but within wonderful communion, day by day, he grows more and more into one body with us, until he becomes completely one with us" (*Institutes* 3.2.24). What do you think Calvin meant by that?

47

Revelation 20:11–15 *Then I saw a great white throne and him who was seated on it. From his presence earth and sky fled away, and no place was found for them. And I saw the dead, great and small, standing before the throne, and books were opened. Then another book was opened, which is the book of life. And the dead were judged by what was written in the books, according to what they had done. And the sea gave up the dead who were in it, Death and Hades gave up the dead who were in them, and they were judged, each one of them, according to what they had done. Then Death and Hades were thrown into the lake of fire. This is the second death, the lake of fire. And if anyone's name was not found written in the book of life, he was thrown into the lake of fire.*

Burke's name

An eponym is a word in the English language which has derived its meaning from a person. Perhaps it was something the person said or did or received. For example, the word "begonia," a plant mostly native to the tropics, came from a Michel Bégon. Bégon was a Frenchman who was governor of Santo Domingo during the reign of Louis XIII. When he returned to Europe, Bégon carried a plant back with him and introduced it to botanists. They named the plant "begonia."

A great many eponyms exist in the English language—some famous, some infamous. The word "burke" is not well known. It was coined after William Burke. William Burke was an Irishman who immigrated to Scotland sometime in the early 1800s. A man of dubious character who had an aversion to healthy work, he drifted into the city of Edinburgh looking for free handouts. He found a cheap rooming house in Edinburgh, acquired a girlfriend with the same lazy mentality as himself and looked about for an easy way to make a living. He managed to establish a second-hand clothing business, but it brought in very little money and very little satisfaction to the greedy pair.

Now at this time in history, anatomy, although a tremendously popular subject among medical students, had not yet made great strides. It was the practice of the University of Edinburgh to offer ten pounds for a cadaver. There were a group of people known as "body snatchers." These were men who would brave dark cemeteries and rob graves, digging up newly-buried corpses and cart them over to the university. This grisly occupation gave William Burke an idea. When an old pensioner died of natural causes, a man who lived just down the hall from him in his rooming house, he put his idea into practice. He spoke to William Hare, the owner of the house and together the two men lugged the dead pensioner's body off to the University. Dr. Knox in Surgeon's Square checked the corpse and, satisfied that the man had died of natural causes, paid the men ten pounds. They were delighted and considered the payment easy money.

The two men, William Burke and William Hare, as well as their female counterparts, after some talk together, lost no time in assessing the health of the other renters in the rooming house. When a second elderly boarder became ill, they offered bed-sitting services and impatiently waited for the man to die. They were very disappointed, however, when it appeared that the fellow might recover. In a moment of greed, Burke held the pillow slip over the old man's face who ceased breathing rather quickly. A return trip to Dr. Knox secured another ten pounds.

With no other ill roomers in the boarding house, Burke and Hare devised a plan. Edinburgh, they reasoned between themselves, was a large city and full of poor and needy people. Drifters surely would not be missed should they disappear. Together with their female companions, Burke and Hare cornered an old woman by the name of Abigail Simpson. This poor lady had just trudged the miles from Gilmerton to Edinburgh to collect her pension. They got the woman drunk, took her to a room in the boarding house, applied the pillow slip and traded her off to Dr. Knox for another ten pounds. A few more destitute women followed in rapid succession. Burke and Hare were actually beginning to enjoy themselves, warming to their macabre occupation.

Over time, Burke became rather inventive in selecting prospects for his murderous plan. He took in an old cinder-gatherer, rescued an old woman and her deaf and dumb grandson from prison and invited several prostitutes over to the rooming house. All of these were murdered, murdered callously and cruelly, and each brought in a coveted ten pounds.

Eventually, and inevitably, the four were caught while putting down a woman by the name of Mary Docherty. They were arrested and brought to jail. Hare denied all knowledge of any murders except for the last and gave evidence. Eventually, he and his wife were set free. The trial of Burke and his girlfriend was next. The case against Burke's girlfriend was "not proven," but Burke himself was sentenced to hanging. The actual number of victims was vague, but it was speculated at anywhere from sixteen to thirty people. The general populace of Edinburgh in 1829 was horrified. When William Burke walked from the prison to the place where the gallows had been erected, a crowd of people followed, shouting, "Burke him! Burke him!"

After the hanging, Burke's body was taken to the university and publicly dissected. The professor who dissected it, lectured for two hours on Burke's brain. The following day, the dissected body was publicly displayed on a large, black marble slab in the anatomical theatre and some 30,000 visitors filed past. After this, William Burke's remains were salted and stored in appropriate barrels for future use at Surgeon's Square.

Food for thought

1. The eponym "burke" means "to murder (someone) by suffocation so as to leave the body intact and suitable for dissection." Burke was actually burked himself. But the fact that he was hung, was only the beginning of his eternal trouble. Comment.

2. The greatest eponymous personality is, of course, Christ. If only Burke had linked his name with that Name—if only he had lost himself and his action in that Name—how very different the outcome of his life might have been. With what will your name be associated after your die? Or, more to the point, with whom will your name be associated? Why.

48

Psalm 32:1–2 *Blessed is the one whose transgression is forgiven, whose sin is covered. Blessed is the man against whom the Lord counts no iniquity, and in whose spirit there is no deceit.*

The pardon

Sir George Groves was an Englishman. Talented and versatile, his interests covered many subjects—music, writing, reading, charity work, lighthouse building, as well as many other things. His actual vocation was that of civil engineer.

Sir George visited Cuba sometime during the 1800s when that country was under martial law. Out walking, he passed a crowd of people on the street and, being rather curious, approached them to see what was the matter. Caught up within the group, he was rather shocked to see a man lying on the ground in the centre of the crowd. It was obvious that the fellow had been murdered. Appalled, he stared down at the corpse. The crowd, meanwhile, aware that there were *gendarmes* approaching, backed off and left Sir George standing by himself as he studied the body. The *gendarmes* arrested him and charged him with murder.

Wasting no time whatsoever, the extremely aggressive police force marched poor Sir George, who was protesting loudly, off to prison. Not only that, they immediately tried him, found him guilty and sentenced him to be shot the very next morning at eight o'clock. Sir George, a bit dazed by it all, although he continued protesting, was close to despair. But although he argued for all his worth, bringing up his talents, his wealth, his reputation and his social connections, it was to no avail. The jury who had found him guilty simply because he had been found standing next to the corpse, remained adamant in their verdict.

"Guilty as charged. You will be shot in the morning."

As a last resort, Sir George sent a message to the British consul. The consul, after inquiring into the matter and discovering Groves to be innocent, put on his British uniform and went to the prison in full regalia early the next morning. He found the firing squad not only ready but also about to carry out the death sentence. Approaching the lieutenant in charge, the consul spoke to him.

"I see you are about to execute one of my countrymen?"

He made his voice severe and authoritative.

"Yes," the man replied, not appearing to be intimidated in the least by either the consul's clothes or his voice. "Your countryman has been found guilty of murder."

"I'm interceding for him," the consul replied, drawing himself up to his full height, "and I urge you to delay the execution until your investigations of this matter are more thorough than they have been up to this point."

The officer shook his head, turned and commanded the firing squad to take their place. In great consternation the consul followed, even pulling at the lieutenant's sleeve to get his attention.

"Ready!"

The lieutenant's voice directed the firing squad to stand up straight.

"Aim!"

They all lifted their rifles and took aim.

"Please," the consul tried once more, "Please, could I at least speak a last word with the condemned man before you proceed?"

The lieutenant, surprisingly enough, gave permission. The consul, breathing an inward sigh of relief, walked up to Sir George who, pale but smiling, grasped his hand in a hard grip.

"Bear with me," whispered the consul, "wait for just one moment."

He took from his pocket a folded Union Jack and unfurled it in a flourish. He then quickly spread it over the prisoner. Sir George stood quietly, not daring to breathe. The flag enfolded him. It covered most of his body. The consul then turned and addressed the lieutenant once again.

"Shoot now, if you dare," he said, pointing at the British flag which represented not only him but a nation.

The lieutenant, as it turned out, did not dare and thus Sir George Groves' life was spared.

Food for thought

1. All of us are like Sir George Groves, only we actually find ourselves in a much worse position: it is not that we have been caught standing next to a dead body—no, it is that we are caught standing in a dead body—our own body! Use Bible texts to either agree or disagree with that statement.

2. Were it not for our Mediator, Jesus Christ, we would continue to stand in our dead bodies. Jesus does not spread a British flag over us, but his own blood, so that we can stand alive and innocent before our God and Creator. "There is, therefore, now no condemnation to those in Christ Jesus," we read in Romans 8:1. Are you covered? How do you know?

49

john 1:1–5 *In the beginning was the Word, and the Word was with God, and the Word was God. He was in the beginning with God. All things were made through him, and without him was not anything made that was made. In him was life, and the life was the light of men. The light shines in the darkness, and the darkness has not overcome it.*

Beattie's lesson

About 150 years ago there was a doctor in Aberdeen, whose name was Beattie. Beattie confessed and believed with all his heart in a triune Creator God.

Dr. Beattie had a small son whom he loved dearly. More than anything else, he prayed that his son would confess the name of the Lord Jesus Christ—that the boy would come to understand that "all things were made through him, and without him was not anything made that was made," because in "him was life, and the life was the light of men." Dr. Beattie knew that the all-important truth of confessing God as Creator, was intricately tied to his child's salvation, and in a unique manner he tried to impress this on his small child.

There was a garden behind Dr. Beattie's house. In a corner of this garden, the doctor sowed watercress in the crevices of the moss that flourished there—and he sowed the watercress seeds in the letters of his son's name. He told no one, smoothing over the dirt and leaving no trace of his interference. Watercress takes root quickly and within ten days of the planting, small leaves were peeping up out of the ground. A few days later an astonished child ran up to his father to report that his name was growing in the backyard.

"Surely not!"

The doctor purported surprise and disbelief.

"Yes, father! Indeed! You must come at once!"

The boy pulled his father's hand and dragged him to the spot.

"Yes," the doctor said, as the boy excitedly jumped about, kneeling every now and then to touch the leaves, "Yes, I see that it is your name in the moss. But what of it? It is merely chance, my son."

"Chance?"

The boy was perplexed. He followed his father, as the older man walked back toward the house.

"Chance?" he repeated again to himself, puzzled by the whole matter.

He called out, just as the doctor, already inside, was closing the back door.

"It cannot be chance, Father. It really cannot be."

Dr. Beattie stepped outside again, earnestly looked at the boy and asked him why it should not be chance.

"Because someone must have contrived it so as to produce my name. It could not really happen by chance, Father."

"So you think," replied the doctor, "that what seems to be the letters of your name, could not have happened by chance?"

"Yes," the lad answered very firmly, "I really do think it could not have happened by chance."

"Look at yourself," said the doctor in return, "Look at your hands and your fingers, at your legs and your toes, at your knees and your elbows—are not all these wonderful and useful to you?"

The boy looked, lifting his arms and bending over to feel his legs.

"Yes," he agreed after a moment, "but..."

The doctor interrupted.

"Think you," he continued, probing his son's thought processes, "that you came about by chance?"

"No," the boy answered instantly, "that could not be."

And after a moment he added, "Something must have made me."

"And who is that something?" the father asked.

The boy shrugged.

"I do not know."

The father had now come to the point for which he had been aiming. His boy's reason understood that what begins and is formed must have a cause and that what is formed with regularity must have an "intelligent" cause. He next told his son, the delight of his heart, the Name of the Great Being who had made him— who had made not only him but the whole wide world around him.

The child never forgot.

Food for thought

1. What do you think it means that there is a complex solar system? That snowflakes have such intricate designs? And that birds migrate instinctively to places they have never seen?

2. Many scientists are not creationists. They do not look to the Bible for answers to their questions. But, they are convinced that the complexity in blood-clotting and cells, for example, means that there is "intelligent design." How are Christians one step ahead of such brilliant scientists?

50

Proverbs 23:29–35 *Who has woe? Who has sorrow? Who has strife? Who has complaining? Who has wounds without cause? Who had redness of eyes? Those who tarry long over wine; those who go to try mixed wine. Do not look at wine when it is red, when it sparkles in the cup and goes down smoothly. In the end it bites like a serpent and stings like an adder. Your eyes will see strange things, and your heart utter perverse things. You will be like one who lies down in the midst of the sea, like one who lies on the top of a mast. "They struck me," you will say, "but I was not hurt; they beat me, but I did not feel it. When shall I awake? I must have another drink."*
Proverbs 22:4 *The reward for humility and fear of the Lord is riches and honor and life.*

The man who found riches and honour and life

M any years ago in the highlands of Scotland, there lived a man by the name of Donald. Donald was ruled by one thing—that thing was drink. If he had any money in his possession, that money would go toward alcohol. It was worse than that. If he had any little thing to barter—a trinket, a piece of clothing or a few hours work—he would trade those things for a few swallows. And if he walked the streets, his ragged cap was always in his trembling hands, hoping that his begging would move passers-by to give him a few pennies so that he might be able to buy a glass of the liquid he so passionately desired.

But God had elected Donald, dirty and addicted though he was, to eternal life, and so it was that he was moved to attend a lecture one day in a great hall in Inverness. It was cold outside and driven by need to be warm, even if it was only for a few hours, Donald shivered his way up a long queue of men and at length sat down to listen to a speaker—a temperance speaker. Hearing the man extol the virtues of a drink-free life and hearing him berate the evils of whiskey and wine, Donald suddenly felt ashamed. So ashamed, indeed, that he made a vow to stay sober.

For months, Donald was able to keep this temperance vow, living from one small job to the next, knocking on doors, and offering his services to all who would hire a man down on his luck. But his heart being empty of the evil of drink, now sought a new food to fill it. Those who seek, the Bible tells us, will find. And being elected by God, Donald found and accepted his Word through the preaching of a passing minister. New Christian friends came his way. By virtue of their kindness, Donald was able to purchase a few trinkets, a little of this and a bit of that, and began life anew as an itinerant peddler.

Now Donald walked the roads a changed man. He rejoiced in each day and was happy as a renewed creature of Christ. One day he passed through Balmoral and imagined out loud how wonderful it would be if he could obtain the patronage of the queen herself who lived at Balmoral. He stopped and considered how much his selling ability would be enhanced by her support.

"Well, Donald," he said to himself, "it can't hurt to try."

He bravely knocked on the door of Balmoral Castle, a little man with a container full of trinkets hitched onto his back and a smile fixed on his face. Although peddlers were generally sent packing as quickly as they came, for some reason the butler who answered the door saw something honest and endearing in Donald. He heard his request, nodded and spoke.

"Follow me."

Through great, long corridors and halls Donald plodded, carrying his box of trinkets under his arm now. They reached a waiting room of sorts.

"Sit down," the butler commanded, though not unkindly, and

Donald sat. He sat on a cushioned chair and carefully held his box on his lap. Not long afterward, a man dressed in fine and rich clothes walked in. Donald rose immediately, almost dropping his box on the floor.

"I understand," the man said, quizzically taking in the poor peddler, "that you want to sell her Majesty some…some trinkets?"

The question, even as the man posed it, seemed ridiculous to Donald who expected to be sent packing as soon as he had nodded his assent.

"I am the Earl of Carlisle," the man went on, adding, "the Minister of State, who takes care of her Majesty's affairs, and to whom might I have the pleasure of speaking?"

"To Donald, the peddler."

The strange providence of it all was, and providence it was, that Donald found favour in the earl's eyes.

"I will recommend you to her Majesty."

The earl nodded, turned and left Donald waiting once again.

So it was, not too many hours later, that her Majesty, the queen, met with Donald the peddler, who stalled out his trinkets on an oaken table in her sitting room. She looked here and there; she touched this and that; and bought a great deal with a gracious, royal smile on her lips. Not only that, she also gave Donald permission to wear the royal arms as the Queen's Peddler. Thankful and glad, Donald left her presence. But while walking down the long corridor, following a liveried servant, he was stopped by the Earl of Carlisle who led him to his own room.

"You have had a good day, sir," the Earl began, as Donald stood in front of him gazing at tapestries on the walls and feeling the wealth of a thick carpet under his feet.

"Before you go on your way," the Earl went on, "I should like you to toast the queen's health with me."

He turned and poured red wine into two crystal glasses, speaking on to the man behind his back.

"You have shown great initiative in coming here; you have an honest face and will do, I think, well in life. Would that more men had such initiative."

He turned and held out a glass to Donald. Donald's heart raced at the sight of the sparkling, rich liquid in front of him. Surely he had never drunk such expensive, well-aged wine. It invited him; it cajoled him; and it laughed at him

"Come now, man! Take it! It's not everyone who drinks to the queen's health in my apartments."

There was a note of irritation in the earl's voice. Donald heard it. And then Donald prayed. He prayed that God would help him overcome the temptation before him and that the earl would understand.

"My Lord," he said, clutching his box, "please excuse me. I cannot drink the queen's health in wine, but I will drink it in water."

"Why?"

"My Lord," Donald said once more,

> I was a drunkard once. I became an abstainer and, by God's grace, I became a Christian. But I know that should I taste such a drink as you hold out to me, my appetite would be revived. You see, my appetite is not dead, but dying and I should likely become a drunkard again should I taste wine. God will support me in the path of duty and that path is to say 'no' I will not take the wine.

The earl looked keenly at Donald and then, after an interminably long moment, smiled.

"You are to be commended," he said, and it will afford her Majesty great satisfaction to know that she has among her loyal subjects one, who in the midst of temptation, can maintain virtue and honour."

Food for thought

1. Everyone has sins—vices, if you will. What vice do you have, or did you have, which you have given up for the sake of being a child of God?

2. 1 John 5:4–5 says: "For everyone who has been born of God overcomes the world. And this is the victory that has overcome the world—our faith. Who is it that overcomes the world except the one who believes that Jesus is the Son of God." How would you explain this text in light of the fact that Donald overcame his drunkenness?

51

Proverbs 19:5; 21:28

A false witness will not go unpunished,
  and he who breathes out lies will not escape.
A false witness will perish,
  but the word of a man who hears will endure.

Your sin will find you out

The Castle of Montargis stands in France. In the great hall of the castle there was once a stone mantlepiece of rare workmanship with a strange scene carved upon it: a sculpture of a dog—an English dog. The question of how this sculpture came about is answered by the following story from the 1300s.

A gentleman by the name of Aubry de Montdidier was travelling through the Forest of Bondi when he was attacked by a robber. He was cruelly murdered and his body was buried beneath a tree. Montdidier's dog, an English bloodhound, escaped death. Although he loyally tried to defend his master, his bravery was to no avail. The murderer left the scene of his crime, but the dog did not. For days, the animal guarded the crude and swiftly dug grave. At length, however, hungry and dejected, he arrived at the house of his dead master's friend. Howling at the door, the dog made such a spectacle of himself that all wondered what the matter might be. Letting the animal in, they fed the emaciated creature. Not content with the food, however, the bloodhound ran back and forth, from hearth to the door and back again, over and over, pulling at the friend's sleeve, entreating the man to follow. The dog's persistence prevailed, and the friend took his servants and followed the dog into the forest. The animal showed no hesitation and after a long trek, led the party to a particular tree. Scratching the earth, the bloodhound's mournful howl sent chills up their spines and one of the group was sent back for a shovel. The subsequent digging revealed Aubry de Montdidier's body.

After this time, the dog lived with the friend, and it so happened that the robber, or assassin, whose name was Macaire, visited the house one day. When the dog beheld the man, he flew at his throat and had not several servants pulled the animal back, Macaire would have died. It should be noted that, on the whole, the dog was endowed with a very gentle nature. The children of the house romped with him and ladies petted him frequently. A lamb could not have been more mild. It was only when he saw Macaire, who continued to visit from time to time, that he became violent. The friend pondered on this. He reflected on the dog's conduct and the animal's obvious love for his late master Aubry. It was a fact that with the bloodhound's unerring guidance the grave had been uncovered. And it puzzled him exceedingly how a dog with such a sweet nature could harbour such an obvious hatred for Macaire. He spoke to others about the unusual circumstances and about the fact that he mistrusted Macaire. In the long run, the story reached the ears of the king—Louis VIII.

Louis VIII, very much interested in the story, had the dog brought to him. He then sat with the creature in a room for some time. The dog was quiet, obedient to commands and playful. But as soon as Macaire was escorted in, on orders of the King, the hair on the dog's back bristled, his fangs showed and he leaped toward the man in such fierceness that it took several soldiers to hold him back from killing the fellow.

Louis was even more intrigued now and became convinced there was something unusual in the fact that Aubry's dog felt this hatred. He consequently commanded that a battle should be fought to determine Macaire's innocence before God of the murder of Aubry de Montdidier. It mattered not that Macaire pleaded not guilty, and that he swore with tears that he had not killed anyone.

"I stand by my decision," Louis VIII said to the accused and to his courtiers, "of battle—battle between Macaire and the dog. It shall take place," he went on, "on the Isle of Notre Dame."

He thought for a while before he continued.

"And these shall be the stipulations. Macaire shall be given a great cudgel as a weapon. He shall defend himself with this cudgel and thus prove his innocence. The dog shall be given an empty cask—a house of sorts—to give him a place where he might be sheltered for a moment to catch his breath. Prepare these things, and we will see what will happen."

It did not take long for the king's conditions to be met. And so, shortly afterward, Macaire and the dog were brought face to face. When the dog was loosed, he immediately began to stalk Macaire. Macaire wielded his cudgel carefully, skillfully. But no matter how he aimed and struck, he always missed the bloodhound. The dog leaped, crouched, ran and dodged and avoided every blow that Macaire struck. Eventually Macaire became exhausted. At this point the animal sprang forward, gripped his opponent by the throat and threw him on the ground. Immediately, knowing that he would surely die if there was no intervention, Macaire confessed to the murder of Aubry de Montdidier. The king and the entire court heard the confession and the king motioned that his soldiers should aid Macaire and escort him to the royal dais.

"By your acknowledgement, monsieur," said the king, to the badly frightened and panting man, "you confess to murder. I will spare you the shameful death by a dog, but die you shall!"

A few days later, Macaire was hung on the Isle of Notre Dame. The dog, on the other hand, lived a few years longer and continued to have a good home at the long-time friend of his dead master.

Food for thought

1. 1 John 1:6 says, "If we say we have fellowship with him while we walk in darkness, we lie and do not practice the truth." When all is not right with us, is there a darkness interposed between ourselves and the pure holiness of God? Have you ever experienced such darkness?

2. The truth is that there are no dogs who watch the smaller and larger sins that we commit each day. But there is an almighty and all-seeing Creator God who is aware of all we say and do, down to every petty item of our existence. How important is confession in your life, and to whom do you confess?

52

1 Corinthians 1:27–31 *But God chose what is foolish in the world to shame the wise; God chose what is weak in the world to shame the strong; God chose what is low and despised in the world, even things that are not, to bring to nothing the things that are, so that no human being might boast in the presence of God. And because of him you are in Christ Jesus, who became to us wisdom from God, righteousness and sanctification and redemption, so that, as it is written: "Let the one who boasts, boast in the Lord."*

On boasting

Many years ago in England, there was a get-together in the home of a squire. Among the guests was a youth who had recently inherited some money, a house and a great deal of property. Perhaps Harold, for that was his name, didn't have the good fortune of parents who disciplined him or teachers who taught him the virtues of respect and modesty. As the guests walked about their host's house and admired the gardens, the boy showed himself to be very proud. For, although he had done nothing to deserve his inheritance, he continually spoke of the poor with disdain and made fun of those who had to work for a living. He insulted the servants and showed no compassion for anything or anyone who came into contact with him.

A wiser and much older man observed and tolerated Harold's conduct for a while and tried to think of a way to teach the young lad a lesson. For the evening meal, about twenty guests sat around a table. The older man sat at the bottom of the table and the much younger Harold sat at the top. They faced one another with some eighteen guests between them. The younger man, as he had done that whole day, monopolized the conversation. And through sheer politeness, the rest of the group listened to him.

"At a recent hunting party, my dog jumped higher than all the other dogs..."

"My new double-barrelled gun outshot..."

"My dexterity at catching salmon..."

"My ability to race thoroughbred horses..."

During the entire first course of the dinner, no less than eighteen subjects were discussed—in all the young Harold professed excellence.

As the servants took away the dishes to make room on the table for the second course, it was quiet for a moment. The older man availed himself of that unique moment to address the younger man. He spoke to Harold in a loud voice as he sat across from him at the other end of the table.

"Sir!" he called out, "If you please! From the place where I sit, which, as you note, is quite some distance away from you, I didn't hear accurately all the anecdotes you were relating. Permit me to ask you: Whose dog was it that jumped higher than all the others?"

"Why, sir," answered Harold blithely and proudly, "it was mine."

The older man continued.

"And whose gun outshot?"

"Mine, sir."

"And who caught the salmon so dexterously?"

"I did."

"And who was able to race so well?"

"I was."

Harold's short answers, although boisterous and booming at the onset of the questions, grew unmistakably softer as the older gentleman, with utmost politeness, went on painstakingly through all eighteen subjects.

The conversation ended with, "So you were both the chief actor and the chief author of all these moments? Is that not so?"

Almost imperceptibly, Harold nodded. A faint blush had appeared on his cheeks. The older man went on, not sparing him.

"Is it not impolite, young friend, to so raise yourself up before the eyes of all present?"

There was no response. And, during the second course of the meal the young man continued to be quiet. The next day, Harold left that home—and it was reported he had been cured of boasting.

Food for thought

1. Why do you think the phrase, "proud as Lucifer" was coined?

2. John the Baptist, when he was testifying about Jesus, said of him, "He must increase, but I must decrease." What does this mean and how can you apply this to your own life?

53

Hebrews 4:9–13 *So then, there remains a Sabbath rest for the people of God, for whoever has entered God's rest has also rested from his works as God did from his. Let us therefore strive to enter that rest, so that no one may fall by the same sort of disobedience. For the word of God is living and active, sharper than any two-edged sword, piercing to the division of soul and spirit, of joints and of marrow, and discerning the thoughts and intentions of the heart. And no creature is hidden from his sight, but all are naked and exposed to the eyes of him to whom we must give account.*

Striving to enter

This story is about Lord Braxfield, who lived during the 1800s and was a Scottish Lord of the Session. That is to say, he was a judge of the court. One autumn Saturday, the court met in a small country town where the assizes were held—a periodical court session for the local administration of civil and criminal justice. The members of the court worked hard most of that Saturday and then adjourned until the following Monday. At the close of the meeting, one of the jury members came up to Lord Braxfield with the request that he be allowed to go home.

"Go home? No, but please stay and dine with us," was Lord Braxfield's reply.

"All right," said the juror, "But I trust you will allow me to go home after dinner."

There were many members of the court present for dinner—judges, jurors, lawyers and magistrates. They all sat side by side, eating, drinking and chatting amiably about home, work and politics. Shortly after the last dish was cleared away, the juror reappeared at Lord Braxfield's side, restating his petition to be dismissed to go home.

"What is your hurry?" Lord Braxfield asked him, "Why not stay here and do your duty to your country, as the other men are doing?"

"Lord Braxfield," the man answered, "I'll tell you. I'm a wealthy farmer and a good deal of my corn is cut down. Because of the bad weather we have been having, however, much of it is in bad condition. For the last two days, the weather has much improved. By tomorrow, I'm sure it will be ready to take in."

"You mean," Lord Braxfield responded, "that you will force those who work for you to labour on Sunday?"

"Yes, I do," replied the juror, not at all abashed by the question, "and I don't think they could be doing anything better than to take in this corn, for it is, after all, food for man and beast. I think God almighty will be more pleased to see the men working at this, than he would be to see them in church. It is my opinion that in this spell of good weather, everyone in this county should be told to work in the farmyard instead of going to church."

In response to the juror's answer, Lord Braxfield sat up very straight. He eyed the man for a long time in such a way that the icy displeasure of his silence could be felt by everyone. It had become very quiet around the dining table.

"Sir," he said at length, "I think you have no idea what you are saying! Were you to do what you propose, it would, in the first place, violate the law of the country and be punishable by that law. And if the officers of the law close by you did not arrest you, they would not be doing their duty. In the second place, sir, what you are proposing is a gross violation of the commandments of God. It is ridiculous, absurd and foolish to suppose that he would be more pleased to see us breaking his commandments than keeping them!"

He paused for breath and drew himself up even straighter. No one around the table moved. All listened respectfully.

"In the third place," Lord Braxfield continued, "your attitude shows a tremendous distrust in the providence of God. A man who calls himself a Christian should be ashamed of such distrust."

The juror, now blushing, made as if to move away. But Lord Braxfield motioned that he should stay.

"Stand still, sir, where you are! For, indeed, you shall not get away until the business of the court is over in this place."

The juror, rebuffed and angry, drooped back to his place where none would speak with him. A colleague clapped Lord Braxfield on the shoulder.

"I knew your lordship was a great lawyer, but I did not know you were so great a divine."

"As long as I live," Lord Braxfield replied, "I will set my face against unnecessary work on the Sunday. Works of real necessity must be done. If a flood were to occur, and your grain was in danger, certainly you should save it. But for people to take in corn on Sunday when there is no great necessity for it, this is something I hope will never be tolerated in a Christian country."

Food for thought

1. Referring to the creation week and God's rest on the seventh day, the Bible instructs us to follow his example. How can you do this?

2. John Newton wrote:

> Safely though another week
> God has brought us on our way;
> Let us now a blessing seek,
> Waiting in His courts today;
> Day of all the week the best,
> Emblem of eternal rest.

What do you think he meant by the last line?

54

Proverbs 2:1–6 *My son, if you receive my words and treasure up my commandments with you, making your ear attentive to wisdom and inclining your heart to understanding; yes, if you call out for insight and raise your voice for understanding, if you seek it like silver and search for it as for hidden treasures, then you will understand the fear of the Lord and find the knowledge of God. For the Lord gives wisdom; from his mouth come knowledge and understanding.*

Calling out for insight

My father, who was a pastor, always said that if he did not ascend the pulpit steps with a great amount of trepidation and fear, there was something wrong. What he meant was that it was important to recognize that preaching was an awesome responsibility —it was a fearful thing to be used as an instrument to tell people what God said. He relied much on prayer, and he prayed before and as he ascended the pulpit steps. "Not many of you should become teachers, my brothers," says James, "for you know that we who teach will be judged with greater strictness" (James 3:1).

This anecdote is about a minister who took James very seriously.

It was very quiet in church one Sunday morning. There had been the usual buzzing and humming of people whispering and moving about. But the bells had been rung, and it was time for the service to commence. Children wriggled, and here and there people began looking at the watches on their wrists wondering why the pastor, a Rev. Bruce, was so long in coming. Five more minutes, ten more minutes, and heads were turning and eyebrows were raised. Finally the beadle, the church officer who usually attended the minister, walked out of the church and crossed over the path leading to the adjoining manse to see if there was something seriously wrong. Perhaps the minister had been hurt and was lying somewhere ill or unconscious.

Coming to the manse, he cautiously entered the front door without knocking. Taking off his shoes, he tip-toed over the carpeted hall to the study. Lifting his hand to knock, he stopped in mid-air. He could clearly hear his pastor's voice. He was speaking with someone. Odd for someone to be visiting at this time, the beadle thought. But then he heard the pastor repeating the same words with some vehemence. He listened, hand still up in the air.

"I protest. I will not go except thou go with me."

The beadle heard that sentence several more times, and presuming that a visitor was with Rev. Bruce, did not feel entirely comfortable about interrupting. He quietly returned to the front door, put his shoes back on and walked out again. Shuffling along the path, he reflected that such things happen: that visitors do show up at odd times and that was just the way it was. Inside the sanctuary, he informed the congregation that their pastor had a visitor who was unwilling to attend services and that Rev. Bruce was trying earnestly to persuade him otherwise. People whispered back and forth for a few minutes, but then fell silent. And they had not long to wait, for but five minutes afterward, Rev. Bruce walked in. He walked in alone, with no visible visitor in tow.

The preaching cut to the heart that morning. It was rich and full and the blessings of the gospel of Jesus Christ were abundant and clear. It was easy for those listening to surmise that the minister had not, after all, entered the sanctuary alone, but that he had been in the company of his Master.

Food for thought

1. Have you ever begged a parent, a friend or a relative to come with you somewhere? What were the tactics you employed? Are they the same tactics you use in prayer when you ask God to be with you?

2. Psalm 105:4 says: "Seek the Lord and his strength, seek his presence continually." It seems that people must seek the Lord, his power and also his company—not just once a week on Sunday, or when we are ill or in some kind of trouble, but all the time. Why do you agree or disagree?

55

2 Corinthians 3:4–6 *Such is the confidence that we have through Christ toward God. Not that we are sufficient in ourselves to claim anything as coming from us, but our sufficiency is from God, who has made us competent to be ministers of a new covenant, not of the letter but of the Spirit. For the letter kills, but the Spirit gives life.*

The letter and the Spirit

During the eve of a battle in the first war of Silesia, Frederick II (1712–1740) of Prussia, also known as Frederick the Great, who had planned carefully where to set up camp and how to protect his site, commanded his men to obey certain rules. One of these rules was that, under pain of death, neither fire nor candle should be lit in or outside the campground after a certain hour. Everyone heard him, and everyone was thoroughly convinced of the gravity of this order. One man, however, chose to disobey.

Captain Zietern, a good officer and faithful soldier, as well as a friend of Frederick, thought to himself that he might have time to write one more letter to his wife. In these uncertain hours, he thought to himself, who knew what the next day's events might bring? So, in spite of his king's strict injunctions, he lit a candle and sat down at the table in his tent.

"My dearest wife," he began, and continued for quite some time to speak in tender sentences of the love he felt for her and his hope of a future time when they would be reunited. Oblivious of the time, he continued to write, paragraph after paragraph. Forgetful of all else, he penned his innermost thoughts and was, therefore, startled when someone lifted the flap of his tent and entered. It was Frederick himself. The letter, which he was about to seal with some wax, fluttered to the floor as Captain Zietern sprang to attention.

"What are you doing?" Frederick said, as the tent flap quietly fell down behind him.

The candle cast Frederick's shadow on the canvas and Captain Zietern frantically tried to arrange his jumbled thoughts. He swallowed with difficulty and knew he was in trouble. He loved his commander, who was also his king, and he blushed that he should have disobeyed the order not to light a candle.

"I was..." he began unsteadily, as he picked up the letter, but did not finish his sentence.

"Were you not aware of my order not to have light?" Frederick asked, half-pitying his soldier, friend and subordinate, half-hoping the man had a logical explanation and excuse.

"I was..." Captain Zietern continued slowly, his blush deepening, "I was writing a letter to my wife."

Even as he spoke, he knew his answer sounded ridiculous.

It was silent in the tent. Contemplating the grim-faced countenance of his sovereign, Captain Zietern knew his reason for lighting a candle had not been good enough for the king. With the letter in his right hand, he threw himself at Frederick's feet and begged for mercy. But he neither could, nor attempted to, deny he had done wrong.

"Stand up," Frederick ordered and Captain Zietern obeyed instantly.

"Sit down," the king said and Captain Zietern moved back and sat down on his chair.

"Add these words to your letter. I shall dictate them."

Captain Zietern unfolded the letter laying it down flat in front of him. He picked up his pen. As the king spoke the words he was about to write, a haze filmed over his eyes, and he repented greatly of the emotions that had given way to his disobedience.

"Tomorrow," the king dictated, "I shall perish on the scaffold."

"Tomorrow," Captain Zietern wrote, "I shall perish on the scaffold."

The king himself sealed the letter.

"It shall be sent," he said to Captain Zietern before he turned to leave his soldier's now dark tent.

Food for thought

1. The fact is that we have written, and continue to write, many letters in defiance of God's orders. The truth is that we have executed, and continue to execute, many actions in our lives that are directly in defiance of God's clear commands. What does this mean with regard to what we deserve?

2. Romans 8:1–4 reads:

> There is therefore now no condemnation for those who are in Christ Jesus. For the law of the Spirit of life has set you free in Christ Jesus from the law of sin and death. For God has done what the law, weakened by the flesh, could not do. By sending his own Son in the likeness of sinful flesh and for sin, he condemned sin in the flesh, in order that the righteous requirement of the law might be fulfilled in us, who walk not according to the flesh but according to the Spirit.

What do these verses mean to you?

56

Psalm 8:2 *Out of the mouth of babies and infants, you have established strength because of your foes, to still the enemy and the avenger.*

The babe's mouth

David Hume (1711–1776), was born in Edinburgh, Scotland. Home-schooled, he was an exceptionally clever child with a mind and wit that outdid many of his own age, as well as those older than himself. He matriculated at the University of Edinburgh and travelled on to France. In France, he turned his mind to writing, and completed a book called *Treatise of Human Nature*, a very skeptical work containing, among other subjects, a chapter on miracles. David did not believe in them. As a matter of fact, he believed in very little. He denied the existence of the individual self, holding that men are nothing but a collection of different perceptions. God does not exist, he said. Nothing exists, he said, except impressions and ideas. Despite having grown up in Knox country and having been bathed as a child in Reformed dust, so to speak, he had no faith. During his lifetime Hume conquered many speakers in masterly arguments, humanly speaking, yet, in the end, it was a child who bested him.

When he was an older man, Hume once dined at the house of a friend. As was the custom, after dinner the ladies withdrew to the drawing-room and the men were left to themselves. As the men conversed together, puffing away at cigars, Hume made a disparaging remark about religion, a remark that clearly illustrated his sentiments regarding God and his creation. Another gentleman chided him.

"If you advance thoughts such as these, sir," the gentleman said, "you certainly are what the world gives you credit for—an infidel."

Now, during the course of this conversation, a little girl had been playing on the floor under the table with her toys. She was a favourite of David Hume, who often, when he visited her parents, brought her toys, candies or little books. When she heard her special friend, David Hume, being called a strange name, she crawled out from under the table, left her dolls lying on the floor and sought out her mother who was in the drawing-room with the female company.

"Mama," she whispered to her, but not so soft that the others could not hear, "Mama, what is an infidel?"

Her mother, in light conversation with the other ladies, stopped talking and focused on her daughter in astonishment.

"An infidel?" she repeated.

"Yes, mama. What is it? I must know."

"Why should you ask such a question?"

"Oh, never mind. I must know."

The little girl persisted in this one question, amid all the smiles and amused glances of the visitors. At length, exasperated, her mother answered.

"An infidel is someone who believes there is no God, no heaven, no hell and no hereafter."

The child's face fell, and she left the drawing-room as quickly

and quietly as she had come. The ladies, after smiling to themselves for a few minutes, resumed their conversations.

A few days later, David Hume visited the household again. He
was shown into the parlour by the butler but found no one there
but the little girl. He smiled and sat down, patted his knee and
invited her to come and sit with him as she had been accustomed
to doing in the past. But the child would not come near him. Her
eyes wide with something akin to horror, she would only stare at
him from a corner of the room.

"What is the matter?" he asked softly, "Why will you not sit with
me? Have I done something wrong? Have I hurt you?"

"No," she replied in a firm voice, not budging from her spot and
not coming one step closer, "You have not hurt me. But I cannot
sit by you, and I cannot play with you any more."

"Why not?"

Hume drew himself up straight, getting exasperated with an
invisible entity he could not see, angry at an invisible hand that
might have blackened his name with the child.

"Why not?" he repeated, as the child just stood there.

"Because," she finally answered, "because you are an infidel."

"An infidel?—and what is that?"

Hume replied with a chuckle and a smug look on his face. He
was quite certain that the child neither knew nor understood the
meaning of the word.

"An infidel is someone who believes there is no God, no heaven,
no hell and no hereafter."

The child responded in a crystal clear and very solemn voice.

"Oh, I see," said Hume thoughtfully and then went on to say,
"and I suppose you must feel rather sorry for me?

"Yes, indeed, I am sorry," replied the little girl, "and I pray to
God for you."

"What do you pray?" he asked, a little taken back but still curious.

"I pray," said the little child, still not coming one step closer,
"Oh, God, teach Mr. Hume what you are."

Then she turned and fled from the parlour, her full little skirt
rustling, leaving behind a man who had heard words of truth
spoken to him in love; leaving behind a man who would never be
able to say he had not been told.

Food for thought

1. In Matthew 11:25 Jesus says, "I thank You, Father, Lord of heaven and earth, that you have hidden these things from the wise and understanding and revealed them to little children." What did he mean?

2. Hume's philosophy was immensely influential and still carries weight with many people today. Do you pray for the many infidels who deny God's all-powerful presence and sustaining providence? How do you do this?

57

Luke 19:24–27 *And he said to those who stood by, "Take the mina from him, and give it to the one who has the ten minas." And they said to him, "Lord, he has ten minas!" I tell you that to everyone who has, more will be given, but from the one who has not, even what he has will be taken away. But as for these enemies of mine, who did not want me to reign over them, bring them here and slaughter them before me.*

Well done

One day an old duke in Scotland bought a cow at the market in a neighbouring town. It was a beautiful day and the duke, who liked to walk through the countryside and enjoy nature, left the cow with the farmer from whom he had purchased the animal, with the understanding that the creature would be driven to his large estate the next day by a hired hand. It so happened that early the next morning the duke, as he was wont to do most mornings, was out for a considerable trek. It rejuvenated him to stroll briskly over the country lanes of his vast property while wearing high boots and plain clothes. At a crossroads several kilometres from his home, he came upon a boy who was having difficulty driving a cow in front of him. When the boy saw the duke, he called out to him.

"Hie, man! Come here and give me a hand with this stubborn beast. She will not do as I say!"

The duke, not quite willing to stop his walk, pretended not to have heard the boy and kept on walking. But the boy, a persistent lad, called louder.

"Hie, man! Are you deaf? Give me a hand!"

But the duke didn't respond, not even by a small turn of his head. He simply kept on walking. Finally, in desperation, as the cow was making for the ditch, the lad yelled out again.

"Come on, man! Give me a hand, and I'll give you half of anything I get to drive this brute to the duke!"

At this offer the duke smiled to himself, turned and retraced his steps to the boy. The lad, glad to have the help, grinned at him. Together they pulled the cow out of the ditch and prodded her back onto the road.

"Now," the duke said, as they trudged along together, "how much do you think you will get for this job?"

"I do not know," the boy replied, "but I'm sure to get something, for the folks up at the house have a lot of money. And it's said they are good to their servants."

When they came, after some time, close to the gate of the estate, the duke slipped away and told the boy he would see him later. Entering the house, he called his butler. Taking out a gold sovereign and clapping it into the servant's hand he told him "Give this to the lad who has brought the cow I bought yesterday at market."

The butler, slightly surprised, nodded and bowed but answered not a word. The duke returned to the end of the lane by the gate and waited for the boy to return. When he did, the duke was not slow to ask him how things had gone at the house.

"Well, how much did you get?"

"A shilling," the boy replied, "and here's half of it for yourself for helping me."

"Surely you received more than a shilling?" probed the duke.

"No," answered the boy, "that's all I got. Do you think it's enough?"

"I do not," answered the duke, "As a matter of fact, I think there's been some mistake."

"Mistake?" the boy repeated after him, standing still.

"Yes, mistake," said the duke, "and as I happen to know the duke, I think we should turn around and go back. It might be that you will earn some more money."

The boy, quite willing to trust his new friend, amiably returned with him to the house. The duke rang the bell himself and, to the astonishment of his small companion, ordered all the servants to be assembled.

"Now," he said to the boy, "point out the man who gave you the shilling."

"It was that man over there. The man with the moustache," replied the boy, pointing to the butler.

The butler fell on his knees, and begged to be forgiven. The duke said nothing but that the dishonest servant should give the boy the sovereign. When this had been done, the duke dismissed the butler from his service.

"You have been given much," he said, "but you have not shared the blessings of your situation. Consequently, you have lost both your character and your situation by your selfishness."

The boy who had stood silent throughout it all, turned over the gold sovereign in his hand with wonder. So pleased was the duke with the young lad's honesty, work and example, that he sent him to school so that he might achieve even more in life.

Food for thought

1. Now we will neither be driving cows through Main Street, nor counting the pounds in our pockets tomorrow for doing so. But we ought to be doing business one way or another for our Lord, not the business of going to Wall Street, of building bridges or of contracting land deals; not the business of procuring PhDs and lofty titles and not the business of scrubbing floors and cooking nutritious meals. Although these things are all important, they are not the tasks which are meant by the parable of the talents recorded in Luke 19. Neither should the amount of the money in the parable trip us up. It's not really that

crucial. What is important is that in this life we all have a job to do—everyone of us. And that job is the proclamation of the gospel! How are you fulfilling this job in your own life?

2. "Well done, my good and faithful servant." If you were to die this year, is that what Jesus would say to you?

58

Proverbs 12:26 *One who is righteous is a guide to his neighbor, but the way of the wicked leads them astray.*

A guide to his neighbour

The book of Proverbs in the Bible is full of admonitions about speaking the truth. Proverbs 12:13 reads, "An evil man is ensnared by the transgression of his lips, but the righteous escapes from trouble." The rewards of being truthful are held up whereas the ways of dishonest words lead only to trouble. Proverbs 12:18 reads, "There is one whose rash words are like sword thrusts, but the tongue of the wise brings healing."

When someone preaches, it is a fact that he should also be preaching to himself. The truths he proclaims and explains should be fixed as tenderly upon his own conscience and heart as he wishes to imprint them on his hearers, his sheep. If his audience is aware that his lifestyle is not in accordance with his words, then he may as well keep silent.

Here is an anecdote about the Bishop of Lichfield to illustrate this fact. Out for a stroll one morning, the bishop breathed deeply of the fresh air and contemplated his fine position as a leader in the church.

"Surely," he thought to himself, "people value my words and look up to me. And that is the way it ought to be."

So engrossed was the man in thinking fine thoughts about himself that he almost tripped over the leg of a fellow seated at the side of the road. Pulled out of his self-absorbed reverie, the bishop stopped and noted to his great surprise, not just one man but six, all miners by the black and smudged look of them, sitting in a companionable half-circle and all eyeing him with a grin.

Although the bishop's first impulse was one of anger because he had almost fallen down, he checked himself and thought it a God-given opportunity to lecture the men on the virtues of honest labour and healthy bodies. He cleared his throat and began to speak.

"What are you men doing here? Should you not all be working? Has the colliery closed down that you should all be sitting here wasting the hours God has designed for honest work?"

They stared at him for a moment and then guffawed a bit. One of their group, a middle-aged fellow, stood up, blackened face shining with goodwill.

"We've been 'loyin', your honor," he said.

"Loyin'?" repeated the bishop, rather surprised, and then, eschewing the dialect, he repeated, "Lying? Why would you be lying?"

"Well, you see," explained the man, not at all discomfited by the situation and still standing right in front of the bishop, "we all here," and he indicated his mates on the ground behind him, "we all here found a kettle, and we've been thinking of who should have it. So we've decided that whoever can tell the biggest loy, he's the one who can take home the kettle. All our wives, you see, your honour," he continued, a bit sheepishly, "would be pleased to own it."

The bishop, peering past the man, saw the kettle. Old but seemingly serviceable, it stood boldly in the middle of the group. For a moment he could see six women, old before their time and weary with much child-bearing, all smiling as their soot-covered spouses brought home this prize. But then the bishop's natural propensity to lecture took over.

"You men should be ashamed," he said, pulling his rich garments about him, "for lying is breaking one of God's commandments."

Then all stared at him and did not reply. He clasped his clean, ringed fingers over one another and continued.

"And the punishment for breaking a commandment will pursue each and every one of you if you do not desist. Lying is an awful offence in the eyes of God."

The men looked from him to the kettle and back to one another again, but answered not a word. The bishop knew he was gaining ground. He felt that this group of sinners in front of him, these men shirking work, responsibility and truth, were being touched to the core. Their silence surely pointed to shame. He pointed a bejewelled finger to himself.

"I," he said, and he said it solemnly, "I have never told a lie in my entire life."

At this utterance, another one of the men jumped up, turned to his companions and said, with laughter in his voice, "Well blokes, looks like none of us will be taking the kettle home. His honour has just won it!"

Food for thought

1. Why do you suppose that a false tongue has been described by some as the chariot of the devil?

2. Proud thoughts of self generally go hand in hand with putting others down. Do you agree or disagree?

59

Hebrews 11:35–38 *Some were tortured, refusing to accept release, so that they might rise again to a better life. Others suffered mocking and flogging, and even chains and imprisonment. They were stoned, they were sawn in two, they were killed with the sword. They went about in skins of sheep and goats, destitute, afflicted, ill-treated—of whom the world was not worthy—wandering about in deserts and mountains, and in dens and caves of the earth.*

Who was Gaudentius?

There is a ruin in Rome that many tourists come to see. It is the great amphitheatre, colossal and magnificent in stature. Standing in the middle of seven hills, even in its decay the past majesty and immensity of its design are keenly seen and felt. Although the idea of this enormous coliseum was conceived by Emperor Augustus, it was not built until many years later during the reign of the proud and ambitious Emperor Vespasian in the year A.D. 72. He used more than 30,000 workers on the project, but died before the work was completed. Eight years later, during the reign of Titus, the amphitheatre was dedicated. Both Vespasian and Titus wanted this coliseum (the third built in Rome), to outshine all other architectural works in the world. Martial, the poet, declared the amphitheatre to be more wonderful than the pyramids of Memphis or the hanging gardens of Babylon.

The workmen on the Colosseum were captive Jews. Seventy-thousand Jews had been brought to Rome by Titus—women, children and men. You could buy thirty Jewish slaves in a Roman market for one piece of silver. Although many men were sent to Egypt to work in the marble quarries, most of them were kept for the work on Rome's largest project—the Colosseum. They carried material from Nero's old house to the work site—columns, capitals, boulders and masses of brickwork. They worked with a dogged determination, probably unaware that the edifice they were erecting would become an arena of slaughter for many—a place without mercy.

In the end, the structure was an amazing elliptical figure, 188 metres in length and 156 metres in breadth. Raised on 80 immense arches, it rose on four successive orders of architecture to the height of 48 metres. Covering six acres, its outside was adorned with pagan statues. Concave slopes were filled with 60 to 80 rows of marble seats plumped up with cushions. There were 64 vomitories (or doors), which opened to a theatre that could hold 50,000 to 80,000 spectators. The lowest row, the podium, was reserved for senators and foreign ambassadors. The podium, closest to the base of the arena, was secured against wild beasts by a breastwork or parapet of gold or gilt bronze. As well, the arena was surrounded with an iron railing and a canal.

A huge canopy (as protection from rain), could be stretched over the entire expanse from the outer wall. The men who worked this awning, according to historians, numbered in the hundreds and were dressed as sailors. At a signal, these men would roll out sails by means of cords, and these sails would form a massive purple, silk sheet, fringed with gold—a sheet that covered the entire interior. Fountains played throughout the coliseum, and an intricate network of tubes sprayed out delicate perfume onto the spectators. A statue of Jupiter stood in the middle of the arena. As well, mechanics underneath the arena could make it assume different forms, depending on the entertainment. It could appear as an empty field; or it could become a garden of rocks and caverns, and it could also, because of subterranean pipes, convert into a wide lake.

For centuries, it was not known who was the Colosseum's architect. Notwithstanding the fact that the Colosseum was an amazing feat of building, no writer or poet or emperor of that time or later, made mention of who designed it. Although archeologists poured over faded inscriptions and marble slabs, no name was ever discovered. But in the 1700s, during excavations in the Catacombs of St. Agnes, a tomb was found. The marble slab that lay on this tomb bore a crown and a palm, and near it was a phial of blood— all testimonials of martyrdom. A rough inscription praised one Gaudentius as the architect of the Colosseum. The inscription elaborated on the fact that Gaudentius had been the victim of gross ingratitude and that, although his genius had contributed to the glory of the city, his reward had been a cruel death. The (translated) inscription reads:

> Caesar had promised three great rewards, but false and ungrateful was the pagan; he who is the great Architect of the heavens, and whose promises fail not, has prepared for thee a reward of thy virtue—a place in the everlasting theatre of the celestial city.

Gaudentius was obviously a Christian, which explains why no signature of acknowledgement was ever written about him for no public acknowledgement of Christians was permitted. They could not be praised, and they were not capable, so it was said, of anything great or noble. Consequently, no poet or writer dared risk his popularity or life by extolling the virtues of a Christian. Gaudentius, therefore, was buried without pomp or ceremony in a grave in the catacombs. The stone slab that bears the words of his death can still be seen in the subterranean church of St. Martina in the Forum.

We don't know whether Gaudentius became a Christian before or after his architectural feat. We don't know whether God used the witness of the early martyrs to open his eyes and heart. We don't know whether he had time to lament the horror of the human sacrifices that took place in the arena. We don't know if he was the husband of a Christian wife or whether he was the father of children. We don't know whether he was rich or poor. Neither do we know whether his life was cut short by the claws of a ferocious lion or the sharp sword of an executioner.

But we do know that he was part of a large innumerable throng, part of that crowd of people to whom it pleased almighty God to give the martyr's crown. We do know he walked into an arena that he himself had designed and that he died there, unacknowledged and forsaken by those who had admired and used his skill for their own purposes.

Food for thought

1. We may not know who Gaudentius was, but his name is not just written on a marble slab in a subterranean church in the Forum. It is also written in the Book of Life. As such, all those whose names are also written in the Book of Life will meet him someday. For he, as well as they, will be raised imperishable. What does imperishable mean?

2. Gaudentius is faintly reminiscent of another architect, isn't he? An architect who created a work of perfection, and who walked wittingly and willingly into it, and died for it. The ruins of the Colosseum will not be rebuilt, but the renewal that is in store for Christ's creation is unimaginable! Comment.

60

Ecclesiastes 11:9–12:1 *Rejoice, O young man, in your youth, and let your heart cheer you in the days of your youth. Walk in the ways of your heart and the sight of your eyes. But know that for all these things God will bring you into judgment. Remove vexation from your heart, and put away pain from your body, for youth and the dawn of life are vanity. Remember also your Creator in the days of your youth, before the evil days come, and the years draw near of which you will say, "I have no pleasure in them."*

Remember your Creator in the days of your youth

In 1831, a boy was born in County Carlow, Ireland. He was the third son of rather well-to-do parents. They were overjoyed at his birth. That is to say, they *would* have been ecstatic, but for the fact that the child was not sound of limb. That is to say, the boy had no limbs at all—only small stumps where his arms and legs should have been. His mother held him—a tiny torso—and she wept. He was healthy only in his ability to cry, to suckle at her breast and to coo. He could not grasp hold of her fingers with a chubby little hand, for he had no hand.

How the parents wept—the father as well as the mother. Turning his face away from the cradle, where the little bundle that could not kick lay, the father clenched his fists and stamped his own sound feet. Was this child a gift from God? Then he and his wife prayed for the grace to also bring up this child in the fear of the Lord. And so they did.

Mr. and Mrs. Kavanagh, for that was their name, sang, read, prayed and played with the child. They also recruited, over the course of his childhood, many surgeons and doctors, who all tried but to no avail, to extend Arthur's limbs by artificial means. Yet, amazingly, Arthur thrived. The muscles in the stumps he had grew so strong that he was able, as he grew older, to ride a horse. His father had a saddle-chair fashioned for him, and as he sat strapped in the device, smiling with delight, he rode at a decent pace around the courtyard. Then, after a time of practice, he rode into the fields of the countryside, even jumping fences. His body breathed with the horse, and he gloried in the freedom of the galloping legs taking him about. Not only that, but he persuaded his parents to let him hunt. While seated on the horse, he would rest a gun on the stump which would have been his left arm, and pulled the trigger with a device attached to his right arm. As well, Arthur Kavanagh fished, learned to write and paint pictures.

Not neglecting the spiritual aspect of his son's education, his father hired a tutor, Rev. David Wood, to teach Arthur. What the boy lacked in physical strength, he made up for in mental ability. His love for God grew strong, his prowess in languages was remarkable and his wit and humour made it a pleasure to be in his company.

In his teens, Arthur travelled extensively with his older brother. They visited Russia, Persia and Indonesia. An expert horseman by this time, much of Arthur's journeys were on horseback. During a trip to India in 1851, at the age of twenty, he was part of a hunting party. Separated for a while from the others, he came face to face with a tiger some ten paces in front of him. Not panicking, he leaned his rifle on the stump of his left arm and shot. The tiger was killed instantly.

Both of Arthur's brothers died while they were still relatively young, making Arthur the sole heir of the family estate in County Carlow, Ireland. With a heart full of love and compassion for the tenants under his care, Arthur took up his role as landlord. Rebuilding homes where needed, gentle and without reproof when tenants were unable to come up with the necessary rent due, he was much beloved. Daily carried about the grounds of the manor house on the back of a servant, his demeanor was always cheerful and never mean-spirited. Appointed Justice of the Peace and Sheriff of Kilkenny County, he often sat under an oak tree close to his home, giving advice and arbitrating justice for the people in the county.

In 1866, when he was thirty-five, he was elected to the British Parliament, remaining there until 1880. It was a most unusual sight to see his miniature body among the great assembly of law-givers—a small body not shy about giving large opinions and never shirking work.

Arthur Kavanagh also wrote letters describing his travels. These accounts were interesting and taught people a great deal about places they had never seen, but places he had visited. One of the most extraordinary letters Arthur Kavanagh ever wrote was one in which he extolled God for his constant goodness, expressing amazement at all the great blessings God had seen fit to bestow in his life.

Arthur Kavanagh died in 1889 at the relatively young age of fifty-one. Although he had been very small of stature, God had given him a big measure of grace. Arthur had sought the Lord in the day of his youth, and it stood him in good stead all the days of his life.

There is a story told of a Quaker who lived in Paris and who, at the turn of a new year, offered a choice of gifts to four healthy young men whom he had employed in his household. The young men could choose either fifteen francs or a copy of the Bible.

"I do not know how to read," said the first, "so I'll take the money."

Silently the master handed him the francs.

"I can read," said the second, "but I do believe the money will aid me more presently."

He too received the francs. The third young man hesitated, but then without any words reached for the money container.

The last of the workers, a young boy only about thirteen years of age, looked at the Quaker. The Quaker repeated his offer.

"You may take the francs," he said, "or you may choose Scripture. It is as you will."

"Well," the boy said, "you have told us the book is good, so I think I shall take it home and read from it to my mother."

The master smiled and handed him the Bible. Taking hold of it, the boy, in a spurt of curiosity, opened its pages and a gold piece worth forty francs fell out onto the floor.

This is how the story goes, and those of us who rejoice in the Bible truths rejoice in the fortune of this lad. We hope he not only used the forty gold francs but also discovered the treasure hidden in the pages of the Bible.

Food for thought

1. Interestingly enough, statistics show that conversions before the age of seventeen are much higher than those after that age. The more a person becomes fixed in his ways, the harder it is to change. It is never too late to accept Christ, but upon death, there is no more opportunity. How are you teaching the children in your house and neighbourhood to remember their Creator in the days of their youth?

2. We are all disabled, when we are born. Our limbs might not be missing, as they were in the case of Arthur Kavanagh, but our spiritual condition is bad. We are, as Ephesians 2:1 says, dead in our sins. Why is it important to know that we are spiritually dead?

61

Proverbs 1:1–6 *The proverbs of Solomon, son of David, king of Israel: To know wisdom and instruction, to understand words of insight, to receive instruction in wise dealing, in righteousness, justice and equity; to give prudence to the simple, knowledge and discretion to the youth—Let the wise hear and increase in learning, and the one who understands obtain guidance, to understand a proverb and a saying, the words of the wise and their riddles.*

Christians or simpletons?

There are always many people willing to offer advice on common, everyday life. Information on anything, the treatment of warts, the care of roses, the secret of youthful skin, the investment of money, seems to be available in brochures, magazines and on the Internet. When our children have physical problems, we go to the doctor; when they misbehave, we have access to numerous counselling facilities; and when they seem stuck spiritually, we send them to the minister.

Often forgotten and gathering dust, is that ageless book of wisdom literature. This book, Proverbs, presents advice on practical everyday matters. It deals with behaviour and attitudes as it seeks to drive home truth and turn people from evil ways.

A story is told of a man crossing a stretch of water on a ferry on a very stormy night. The water was extremely rough, the waves were very high and the wind severe. It was a great struggle for the fellow to get to the other side. When he got home, his wife was very glad to see him.

"Ah, George," she said, "Providence has been very good to you."

"Yes, sweetheart," he replied, "but I was pretty clever myself as well."

Proverbs 26:12 admonishes, "Do you see a man who is wise in his own eyes? There is more hope for a fool than for him."

John Kerr (1830–1916), related the following story concerning two old pastors who had served as colleagues in the same church for many, many years. They were, in spite of a host of differences, quite fond of one another and expressed amazement to one another that, in spite of these differences, they had been able to remain colleagues for more than thirty years without quarrelling. This had been, they agreed, totally a matter of good fortune.

"But," said the first, "we have not really done that well, for our church, on most Sundays, is quite empty."

"Ah," rejoined the other, "but again you can see good fortune here. Being colleagues, we have nearly emptied one church; if we had had separate charges, we would have nearly emptied two."

Then, still in a serious vein, they continued.

"I find it more tiring to listen to a sermon than to preach it," said the one.

"Yes," replied the other, "I agree. I have often been more fatigued hearing you preach than when I preached myself."

"Exactly," said the first, "which shows it's a great pity for them who must hear us both."

Proverbs 10:14 responds: "The wise lay up knowledge, but the mouth of a fool brings ruin near."

During the 1700s, a lady once had her portrait painted by one of the most distinguished artists in Paris. She was very beautiful and quite vain. She sat for the artist, posing and smiling, smug about her appearance and her expensive dress. The lady was not as young anymore as she might have liked. As a matter of fact, although she never would have admitted it, she was just past fifty. Not that anyone would have guessed. She used powders, ointments and dyes, and thus skillfully hid wrinkles and age spots.

The artist, skillfully depicted her, but he did not hide the fact that she was an older woman. When he was done, he presented her with the painting—a striking likeness. She gazed at it and became furious. She despised the reality of the mirror image. Stamping her foot, she insisted the picture was not her and left in a huff, refusing to pay the 3,000 francs upon which they had agreed.

The painter was not only insulted but also very angry. He had been slapped in his face, as it were, with regard to his talents and neither would he be able to take any money to the bank. Therefore, he resolved upon an idea. There was to be an exhibition of paintings at the Louvre. He told friends to tell the lady whose likeness he had drawn, that her picture would be shown at the exhibition.

The woman, upon hearing that the picture would be exhibited, came back to knock at the painter's door. He opened, smiled, bowed and let her in.

"Where is the picture?"

He walked to his atelier and came back with the canvas. He held it up so that she could see it. Aghast she stared at it.

"What have you done?"

The portrait was the same, but the artist had thinned her hair, and he had put two false tresses of hair in the lady's hands; as well, he had put several bottles of cosmetics next to her entitled "White-wash," "Vegetable Red," "Wrinkle Remover" and "Hair Dye."

"This is abominable," the lady cried.

"Why?" the artists asked calmly, "Didn't you say when you left the last time you were here that it was not your portrait? Well then, what is the problem? I am quite happy to hang this picture on a wall in the Louvre at the exhibition."

The lady almost exploded with rage.

"What? You are going to exhibit this?"

"Certainly," he answered with a smile, "and I shall entitle it, 'Coquette at age fifty-five'!"

The lady almost passed out with rage, but reached for her purse and paid the 3,000 francs that had been agreed upon, after which the artist effaced what had been added.

Proverbs 31:30 reads, "Charm is deceitful and beauty is vain, but a woman who fears the Lord is to be praised."

Food for thought

1. Will merely knowing or mouthing proverbs make you wise? Why or why not? Is becoming wise a hard, continuous, sweaty, back-breaking process? How so?

2. Proverbs offers practical guidelines and must be read prayerfully and on a continuous basis. It is a vital key to becoming wise. Little proverbs —little wisdom. Christians or simpletons? Comment.

62

Psalm 40:1–4 *I waited patiently for the Lord; he inclined to me and heard my cry. He drew me up from the pit of destruction, out of the miry bog, and set my feet upon a rock, making my steps secure. He put a new song in my mouth, a song of praise to our God. Many will see and fear, and put their trust in the Lord. Blessed is the man who makes the Lord his trust, who does not turn to the proud, to those who go astray after a lie!*

The pit

In 1942, the Germans advanced on the small town of Tsirkuny in the Ukraine. The people of Tsirkuny were understandably apprehensive and mobilized their young men to defend the town.

Mr. and Mrs. Sivalenko lived in Tsirkuny. Like all the other people in Tsirkuny, they were terrified for their loved ones. They were especially worried that their oldest child, a nineteen-year-old son named Grisha, might either be arrested or shot while serving on the small defense force drafted by the town council. They also had a much younger son, but did not think the Nazis would trouble to single him out. And in the dead of night, Mrs. Sikalenko conceived of an idea, an idea she shared with her husband and with Grisha the next morning as she served them breakfast. "We have a goat shed," she announced triumphantly, as she ladled out the steaming porridge, "and who would think to look into a goat shed?"

Mr. Sikalenko and Grisha looked at her doubtfully, not comprehending her meaning. Grisha put a spoonful of porridge into his mouth and his father repeated his wife's last words.

"A goat shed?" he said, "and what has that got to do with anything?"

"Don't you see," Mrs. Sikalenko went on, "that if Grisha hid there, he could burrow under the manure pile at the back."

"They'll look for me, mother," the practical lad answered, "and a goat shed is not a hard thing to search."

"True," she went on determinedly, "and that is why you must first march out to war with the boys of Tsirkuny before the Nazis arrive. That way everyone will think you are gone, and no one will look for you at all. And if they should look for you," she repeated again, "why, who would look under the manure pile in the goat shed?"

Grisha was no hero. Dreams of fighting for his fatherland did not course through his veins. Rather, nightmares of being shot, hunted down and tortured typified many of his sleeping hours.

"All right," he conceded to his mother, "I'll do it."

And so he did. The very next day he marched away with a group of village youths. But later that evening, under the cover of darkness, and already under fire by enemy troops, he deserted and safely made it back to his parents' house. His mother led him into the back of the goat shed.

"Don't mind the goats and the dung," she told him, "at least you'll survive."

Twice a day Mrs. Sivalenko brought her son food, although she rarely stopped to chat. And so the war wore on. In the shed, Grisha had ample opportunity to reflect and think. He felt safe for a while, then lonely and then angry at God for creating a situation as dismal and horrifying as his dung pit. His anger and fear festered, making him sink lower and lower into despair. Where was God and who was he, after all? And if he was sovereign, why had he allowed Nazis to descend into the lives of peaceful citizens like his family?

Springs, summers, autumns and winters touched Tsirkuny. The years passed on. In the winters, Grisha nearly froze. It was extremely cold in the cavity he had dug out underneath the dung heap. In the summers, when the hot sun beat down on the refuse, he almost suffocated with the heat. But he had gotten used to the rotten smell of his surroundings. In the village of Tsirkuny, word was out that those young men who had not returned home over time, had died a hero's death fighting the Germans. Grisha Sivalenko had not returned, or so they thought, and his name was likewise remembered and celebrated as a fallen hero. They praised him in passing as one of those selfless young men who had given his life for his village and for his country.

It was only on very dark nights that Grisha could summon enough courage to venture outside. The war had been over for a long time. Grisha's mother continued to feed her son but could not induce the boy, now a man, to leave his dung pit. Grisha had turned into a self-imposed recluse. He feared open spaces. More than that, he feared what people would think and do if they were to meet him on the street. One night, as he crawled out of his self-imposed exile, he saw crosses on the housetops of Tsirkuny. Mistaking TV aerials for signs of doom, he quickly returned to his pit. He felt that God would surely punish him for having fled from what he now, after much thought, perceived had been his duty.

The day came when Grisha's younger brother got married. Grisha, in his dung cavity, could hear laughter and merry-making all around the house, and he bitterly rued the day when he had sought refuge in his hiding hole. He finally realized that cowardice had induced him to be buried alive. Yet it still took him several months to summon up enough courage to face daylight permanently. He feared that his desertion, now eighteen years past, would be grounds for the village council to have him shot. Yet the solitude and guilt were more than he could bear, and suddenly one day he emerged from the dung pile, shouting at the top of his lungs:

"I want to live! I want to work!"

Brought before a village tribunal, Grisha Sivalenko was not prosecuted for his desertion. The men felt that eighteen years in a manure pile had been punishment enough. What consequently happened to the man, is not known.

Food for thought

1. If you had met Grisha in the week after he had emerged from the dung pile, how would you have counselled him in his despair?

2. The mercy of God ordains all things. It cannot be stressed enough that God is sovereign, even in a dung-heap, and can work all things for good. Comment.

63

Proverbs 31:28a *Her children rise up and call her blessed.*

A godly mother

I n 1837, in the town of Northfield, Massachusetts, a small baby boy was laid in the arms of Betsy Moody. Edwin, the father, a stonemason who also cultivated two acres of land to feed his growing family, looked on proudly. The baby, whom they named Dwight, was the sixth son. Edwin Moody and Betsy Holton were both descendants of the Pilgrim Fathers who had crossed the Atlantic in search of freedom of worship.

Edwin died at the relatively young age of forty-one, leaving behind seven sons and two daughters. Betsy gave birth to twins, a month after he died. Friends and relatives encouraged her to give up her children, as she would, they implied, undoubtedly be unable to raise them alone. She refused to do so.

"I trust in the Father of widows," she said, and her children heard her, "and in him who is the Father of the fatherless."

Edwin had been unfortunate in business and soon after his death creditors took everything—even the kindling wood. It was so cold in the little house, Betsy told the children to stay in bed to keep warm until it was time for school. There was prayer, much prayer on her part—prayer for help. Then an uncle brought a load of firewood, a large load. The house was warmed, and again there was much prayer—prayer of thanksgiving.

Trusting in God was Betsy's creed and she passed it on to her children. She also never turned away the poor from her door. Once when a beggar came, she put the situation to her children and offered them the opportunity of sharing what little they had. They all volunteered to have their slices of bread cut thinner so that the man could eat with them.

She disciplined with a rod. If Dwight disobeyed, there was no time out, no excuse. He was spanked and that was all there was to it. She would send him out for a rod—a branch or a stick. If he brought her a dead one, she would snap it and tell him to get another. She was not in a hurry, certainly not when she was whipping a child. Once Dwight told her that it hadn't hurt at all, but he never had occasion to say this again, for she put it to him so hard that it did hurt. She believed, as the Bible clearly states, that folly was bound up in Dwight's young heart, and that the rod of discipline would drive that folly far from him.

Betsy trusted God implicitly and passed this on to her children. Once when Dwight was eight he worked on a neighbouring farm with his brother during harvest season. On their way home they had to cross the Connecticut River by ferry. Crossing the fields, hand in hand, the young boys approached the landing, hailing the ferryman on the other bank. He came but was quite drunk and, as they found out on the swiftly flowing current of the river, unable to row properly. As the rushing water carried them downstream, they became alarmed—downright scared. Dwight took the hand of his older brother and tried to cheer him up.

"Remember what mother says," he said, "God always watches

over us and protects us from danger no matter where we are."

They landed safely on the other side, strengthened in faith.

On another occasion, Dwight worked out in a farm field with a young man. He was only a lad at the time.

"My mother," said the man as he hoed and pulled the implement back and forth, "gave me a text."

"What was it?" Dwight asked.

"It was," said the man, "Seek ye first the kingdom of God."

He fell silent and worked more until, after the space of some five minutes, he continued.

"I didn't listen to my mother."

Clods of earth flew this way and that. Dwight working alongside didn't know what to say. He thought of his own mother and how he did not always listen to her, and felt a twinge of conscience. She often prayed for him, he knew, and didn't hesitate for a moment to punish him when he did something wrong. He knew it was love that made her do it.

"One Sunday," the man suddenly continued, "I went to church and the text the minister preached on was the same as the one my mother had told me to keep."

"Seek ye first the kingdom of God?" Dwight asked.

"Yes," the man affirmed, "seek ye first..."

Again it was quiet for the space of a few minutes.

"My heart," said the man, as he put down the hoe and wiped his face with a rag, "my heart was not soft—not soft like this earth. I was determined to first seek wealth and to stop attending church. But the text," and here he looked Dwight full in the face, "the text haunted me. It followed me. For I did attend one other service and the minister there again preached the words 'Seek ye first the kingdom of God.'"

"What happened," Dwight asked in spite of himself.

"I did not go back to church until my mother died. And then I resolved, indeed, I had made up my mind to become a Christian. But my heart," and the man pointed to his broad chest, "my heart was like a stone."

At this point, he dislodged a stone with his hoe, picked it up and hurled it away.

Years later, Dwight asked his mother what had happened to the man. She told him the man had become insane. Dwight asked for his address and looked him up. The fellow was sitting on a rocking chair on his porch and as soon as he saw Dwight approach, he lifted up his hands toward the sky and spoke.

"Seek first the kingdom of God, young man," his voice rang out, "Seek first the kingdom of God."

Other people informed Dwight that these were the only words the man ever spoke, and that he spoke them to all who approached him.

Betsy Moody inspired devotion. Even after Dwight was absorbed in evangelism, he wrote to his mother frequently and gave her an account of all the things going on in his life. When she died, he wrote:

She made home so pleasant! I thought so much of my mother, and cannot say half enough. That dear face—there was no sweeter face on earth! Fifty years I have been coming back and was always glad to get back. When I got within fifty miles of home, I always grew restless and walked up and down the [rail] car. It seemed to me as if the train would never get to Northfield. For sixty-eight years she lived on that hill and when I came home after dark I always looked to see the light in my mother's window. It was because she made our home so happy that she started me thinking how to make happy homes for others.

Food for thought

1. Dwight Lyman Moody (1837–1899) didn't have much of an education but by God's grace, he became an evangelist and preached the gospel to probably more than a million people. How did God use his mother?

2. What are some characteristics that you feel will make a child call a mother blessed?

64

Jeremiah 5:22 Do you not fear Me? declares the Lord; Do you not tremble before Me? I placed the sand as the boundary for the sea, a perpetual barrier that it cannot pass; though the waves toss, they cannot prevail; though they roar, they cannot pass over it.

Boundaries

There are boundaries throughout all of life—boundaries in the world of nature as well as in the world of man. God, the Creator of everything in the universe, has made things in such a way that nothing is outside of his control.

Yacht racing was a sport enjoyed by the German kaiser Wilhelm II (1859–1941). At Kiel Fjord, an area wrested by Germany from Denmark in a previous war, he established a space where he could indulge in that sport. The area was lined by huge granite cliffs and dark green forests—an awesome setting for a summer regatta.

Wilhelm invited wealthy people—people such as the American millionaires J.P. Morgan, Cornelius Vanderbilt and Andrew Carnegie—to participate. Flattered to be remembered by an emperor, they usually accepted the invitation.

In 1904, an American millionaire by the name of Morton F. Plant came to Kiel for the annual regatta. His boat, *Ingomar*, was easily the fastest ship there. Skippered by the finest American racing captain of the day, Charlie Barr, she competed against the *Meteor III*, the yacht belonging to Wilhelm II.

The day of the regatta was a fine day with a good wind. Fifteen boats took part in the first race. But, from the start, it was evident that it would be a race just between *Ingomar* and *Meteor III*. Although *Meteor III* was ahead initially, *Ingomar* quickly began to overtake the imperial yacht with the kaiser on board. The *Ingomar* was on a starboard tack, which gave her the indisputable right of way. But Wilhelm II had no intention of giving way. After all, he was the kaiser. No one spoke on the *Ingomar*. The crew lay flat on the deck. The millionaire, Morton F. Plant, stood on the stairway, his head just above the sliding hatch. He had a cigar in his mouth and his Panama hat was pulled over one eye. The yachts came closer and closer together, and it seemed inevitable that the American yacht would hit the kaiser's ship.

Every stitch of canvas was blown full of breeze, and all the men on board the *Ingomar* were prepared for a good crash. Charlie Barr, the skipper, neither flinched nor budged from his course, and at the last moment the *Meteor* put her helm down and turned slightly. The *Ingomar's* bowsprit was within three feet of the *Meteor's* rigging. Both vessels just missed one another and rushed on in the race. The bluff of royalty the kaiser had erected, had been called by the Americans. And the *Ingomar* won—not only that race but every one it participated in that summer.

There is another story of a ship—a ship traversing through dark and stormy waters—encountering a light, which the master of that ship assumed to be another vessel. He took a microphone and called out.

"Collision imminent. Veer ten degrees north!"

A voice called back over the water, a voice not a whit less lacking in authority than the commander.

"No, you veer ten degrees south."

"I'm an admiral," the first man responded, rather testily, "Now, veer ten degrees north."

"I'm only a midshipman," the second voice called back, "but you must still veer ten degrees south."

In the meanwhile, the light was getting closer and closer.

Disdaining to be frightened, the admiral called out again.

"I'm a battleship. Now veer ten degrees north!"

"No, you veer ten degrees south," the voice replied smoothly, "because I am a lighthouse."

The admiral, admiral though he was, had encountered a law of inanimate rock. Had he pursued his course, he, and his crew with him, would have been hurled into inevitable death. He wisely altered course.

Food for thought

1. If you have ever seen a child in a playpen, you know the child has boundaries assigned to him by his parents to protect him from unknowns. A child is not always happy in a playpen, especially if he thinks that things outside of his quarters would be much more fun and challenging than the area he has been given. In the same manner, God has put barriers, or limits on men and women—on what they can and cannot do. What barriers have you encountered?

2. In 1 Peter 2:8, Jesus is called "A stone of stumbling, and a rock of offense." What kind of people stumble on this rock, and what is their destiny?

65

1 Kings 12:26–30 *And Jeroboam said in his heart, "Now the kingdom will turn back to the house of David. If this people go up to offer sacrifices in the temple of the LORD at Jerusalem, then the heart of this people will turn again to their lord, to Rehoboam king of Judah, and they will kill me and return to Rehoboam king of Judah." So the king took counsel and made two calves of gold. And he said to the people, "You have gone up to Jerusalem long enough. Behold your gods, O Israel, who brought you up out of the land of Egypt." And he set one in Bethel, and the other he put in Dan. Then this thing became a sin, for the people went as far as Dan to be before one.*

False unity

Many people have tried to lure Christians away from their worship. In the last century, Joseph Stalin attempted to seduce millions to worship a human gold calf by the name of Vladimir Lenin (1870–1924). Lenin was the renowned founder of the Russian Communist Party and first head of the Soviet State.

Several months before Lenin's death in January 1924, a secret conference was held by several members of the Russian Politburo. Trotsky, Bukharin, Kamenev, Kalinin, Rykov and Stalin all met to discuss Lenin's failing health. A power struggle was underway, as all were aware that after Lenin's death the reins of power would fall into someone else's hands. On the day of the secret conference, Stalin is reported to have said:

> Comrades, Vladimir Ilich's health has grown so much worse lately that it is to be feared he will soon be no more. We must therefore consider what is to be done when that great sorrow befalls us. I understand our comrades in the provinces are exercised about this matter. They believe that it is unthinkable that Lenin, as a Russian, should be cremated. Some of them suggest that modern science is capable of preserving his body for a considerable time, long enough at least for us to grow used to the idea of his being no longer among us.

Although most of the others in this meeting did not agree with Stalin, his wish prevailed. The "comrades in the provinces," however, were a figment of the imagination, for it was Stalin himself who wanted Lenin embalmed for the masses. Desiring unity under his own leadership, albeit a devilish unity, he saw Lenin's body as a wonderful way to harness religious sentiment, the desire for worship, in the masses. He intuitively knew that if the majority of the Russian people were to turn to God for true worship, his own chances of survival as atheistic ruler were slim.

Consequently, Stalin turned Lenin's death into a golden calf. He spoke to the Russian people, saying:

> Comrades, workers and farmers, men and women, I have an important request to make of you. Do not let your sorrow be transformed into demonstrations of adoration for Vladimir Ilich's personality. Do not put up buildings or monuments in his name. When he was alive he set little store by such things; indeed, he actively disliked them. You know the poverty and disorder that afflict our country. If you want to honor Vladimir Ilich's memory, build creches, kindergartens, houses, schools and hospitals. Better still, live according to his teaching.

That teaching was, of course, atheistic communism under the new leadership of Joseph Stalin.

The "cult of Lenin" was born. After a grandiose funeral was orchestrated, Lenin's body became an affair of state. A mausoleum was built, the name LENIN carved on it in Cyrillic capitals and his body, even though it was already actively decaying, was prepared to be worshipped. The skin on the face and hands had darkened, wrinkles could be seen on various parts of the body and the lips had parted slightly. The eyes had sunk into their sockets, and there were brown marks round the skull where it had been sawn open to extract the brain. (The brain had been transferred to a research institute charged with demonstrating that the father of the Revolution had been a genius.) A concoction was formulated by a small team of scientists to preserve the body. Incisions were made into the body, and it was bathed in a tub containing a solution of glycerine, potassium acetate, water and quinine chloride. This bath was given to the body every eighteen months as a general overhaul.

In time, a second and grander mausoleum was built and scientists continually improved the visible state of the body. By 1934, a few foreigners were allowed to visit and one of them remarked, "I really feel I'm looking at a man sleeping. You find yourself walking on tiptoe so as not to wake him.... The embalming of Lenin is the most perfect example I've ever seen of the art—better even than the mummies of ancient Egypt." Between 1924 and 1940, the mausoleum was visited by more than 16 million people—people who worshipped the dead. It was also during this time that thousands of Greek Orthodox priests were executed or sent to forced labour camps. Some 90 percent of the churches were either destroyed or converted into garages and other structures.

Stalin had gone the way of King Jeroboam, and the ungodly unity he wrought condemns him before the judgement seat of God.

Food for thought

1. How can tradition, rules and regulations be elevated to an improper form of devotion, indeed, to idol worship? What is the only true and pure unity possible among people within the church?

2. It is good to visit a cemetery every now and then—to reflect on all those bodies decaying underneath the gravestones, awaiting the resurrection. All those bodies worshipped something or someone during their lifetimes and are reaping the result of that worship. Comment.

66

Proverbs 3:13–18 *Blessed is the one who finds wisdom, and the one who gets understanding, for the gain from her is better than gain from silver and her profit better than gold. She is more precious than jewels, and nothing you desire can compare with her. Long life is in her right hand; in her left hand are riches and honor. Her ways are ways of pleasantness, and all her paths are peace. She is a tree of life to those who lay hold of her; those who hold her fast are called blessed.*

Riches without understanding

There are those who are rich, and there are those who are poor. Perhaps everyone has said at one point or another, "If only I had a million dollars, I would...." Some of us might have more expensive food, might wear brand name clothing, or might be able to visit places such as Disney World or other places of entertainment. But, the truth is, all of us have access to the one thing that makes us wealthy beyond measure—the Word of God.

A radio program was aired not too long ago in which two ladies spoke together. They were both so fond of their pets that they decided to visit someone holding the dubious title of "pet psychic." The one lady wanted to see this psychic because her budgie had died, and the other wanted help with a dog who seemed to be afraid of the veterinarian.

The interview between the psychic and the two ladies was taped for radio broadcast. Listeners heard the psychic establish so-called "contact" with the dead budgie. In sympathetic and sweet tones, she told the owner that the budgie forgave her for euthanizing him. Bud, the budgie, was now, the psychic told the mesmerized owner, happy in his work as a spiritual guide for children in India.

The psychic went on to analyze the second lady's pet. Charlie the dog, listeners were told, sat quietly, looking intently at the psychic. The psychic, receiving great chunks of pup history by this eye-to-eye exchange, was informed by the dog that he had fallen off a vet's table when only three months old. The psychic relayed to the owner that it had really helped Charlie to be able to talk about his bad experience.

At the end of the relatively short interview, radio listeners were advised that the visit to this helpful and sincere psychic had cost both these pet owners a whopping $100!

So what profit is there in reading this little vignette? The sad truth of the whole ridiculous matter is that from this story we learn that all the people involved were extremely impoverished. They were impoverished in the wisdom and understanding of almighty God—riches to which they had ready access.

The Bible teaches us very plainly that animals are animals and that people are people. The Bible teaches very plainly that God breathed into man—not beast—and gave man a soul. The Bible teaches very plainly that man was put on earth as steward over all creation, and this creation includes animals. Reincarnation is not true for man, and it is not true for animals either. And, animals, unless God so chooses to use them for a specific purpose ordained by him (as in Balaam's donkey), do not speak.

Food for thought

1. How very grievous when people who live in a land of plentiful access to the riches of God, choose to be impoverished. Why do you suppose that people choose to ignore God and his Word?

2. We grin and laugh at the obvious stupidity of people who really want to believe that their animals have characteristics and abilities that match their own. But listen to the wry sense of divine humour and condemnation in Psalm 49:20: "Man in his pomp yet without understanding is like the beasts that perish." What does this text mean?

67

Psalm 49:20 *Man in his pomp yet without understanding is like the beasts that perish.*

The death of a jackal

Long ago, in 246 B.C., to be exact, there lived an emperor who ruled a vast kingdom. He was only thirteen years old at the start of his reign. Young as he was, he conquered and unified many warring states and considered himself to be the first legitimate emperor of his country. Because of this he added Shih Huang-Ti to his own name of Ch'in. ("Shih" because it means first; "Huang" because it means sovereign; and "Ti" because it stands for emperor.) Clearly, humility was not one of his overriding virtues.

Ch'in did not bear any resemblance to a handsome fairytale

Prince Charming. On the contrary, his nose was very large; his eyes were bulbous; his chest was barrel-round, and his voice was so rough and raspy that people said he sounded like a jackal. Still, it is the heart which makes a person what he is. God, therefore, did not look at Ch'in Shih Huang-Ti's outward appearance, but at his inward appearance. Was he noble? Was he courageous? Was he a person who searched for and acknowledged the Creator God?

The young teenager grew into a distrustful man and one who burned ancient classics and records. These records included the *Book of History*, a book in which a Creator God was mentioned. Ch'in also buried alive 400 Confucian scholars who opposed his power structure. As a matter of fact, he was so suspicious of other people that in his capital city of Xianyang he had not just one palace, but 270. These palaces were all connected by private passage ways so that Ch'in could get around without being seen. If he did leave these "safe" passages to go into the city, he always wore a disguise. Anyone unfortunate enough to recognize him (and perhaps his nose was a dead giveaway), was instantly put to death. It appeared that Ch'in was a harsh ruler, and one not overly concerned with the welfare of his people.

Nevertheless, God permitted Ch'in to work out certain reforms in China. The name "China" is derived from the Ch'in dynasty. Ch'in joined together protective stone walls along the northern border to begin what we now know as "the great wall of China." He built watchtowers, garrisons, a vast canal system and better roads. Currency became one stable coin, and justice was carried out with the intention of obliterating crime. Ch'in standardized the writing style of the Chinese characters, and weights and measurements. All these things and more, God permitted Ch'in to accomplish. Whatever a king or emperor does, after all, is in the hand of the Lord. "The king's heart is a stream of water in the hand of the LORD; he turns it wherever he will" (Proverbs 21:1).

Ch'in attained tremendous power through his military victories. Because he was so suspicious, however, his rule was very despotic. For the smallest offense people were flogged, branded, dismembered, buried alive, cooked in cauldrons or decapitated. And if one member of a family offended, the whole family was punished. Because Ch'in was so tremendously unloving and unjust, God punished him by making his life one of ever greater fear and one of continuous warfare. Many people disliked and hated him, and consequently, there were many attempts on his life. There were rebellions in his army and uprisings in many villages. Nomads made holes in the protective great wall and tribes made war on him season after season.

Under the influence of Taoist priests who worshipped many gods and practiced alchemy, divination and magic, Ch'in never sacrificed to one God, but sacrificed to many. Although, humanly speaking, Ch'in was a powerful ruler, it was not easy for him to sleep at night. He was afraid of the dark, and he was also terrified of something else—death. More than anything, he wanted to live and keep his power forever. He consulted magicians and put stock in legends which said that immortal beings lived on three mountains in the middle of the Bohai Sea. Three times he sent out ships loaded with young men and women to find these mountains. For hours he stood gazing out at the sea, hoping for a glimpse of eternity. But the ships never came back and historians speculate that the people Ch'in sent out may possibly have been Japan's first settlers.

Losing hope of discovering a magic elixir that would allow him to live on earth forever, Ch'in began preparing for his death. Utilizing some 700,000 slaves, he built a huge, 500-foot high mausoleum. It had secret passages and anyone acquainted with these tunnels, such as the 10,000 builders who had been directly involved, were buried in it on its completion. Afraid of others even in the death which he knew was inevitable, Ch'in went on to build an army for his tomb—an army of 6,000 clay soldiers. Each soldier was six feet or taller, and each was made differently from the next. There were archers, infantrymen and cavalry soldiers, plus horses and chariots. There were also models of clay slaves as well as furniture for the use of the deceased—for the use of a corpse. For the dead man's eyes, the ceiling of the tomb was painted with stars and constellations. Rivers filled with mercury were drawn on the wall so that they appeared to be flowing on forever. It seemed all Ch'in needed was a good book, a cup of lotus tea and some Chinese take-out for him to have a comfortable existence in his coffin! If by chance someone should succeed in finding his way through the maze of secret passages and also possibly work his way through the terra-cotta army, Ch'in provided a third obstacle. The entrance to his burial chamber was booby-trapped with automatic crossbows. This tomb was discovered in 1974.

All Ch'in's precautions to preserve his life, even in death, were in vain. He, even as all men, began to decay as soon as he breathed his last in 209 B.C., and he faced eternal judgement the moment he died. He died outside his city, and away from his 270 palaces. His body was brought back to Xianyang in a carriage. Because his officials were afraid the people would riot if they found out that the emperor was dead, his death remained a secret for quite a few days. His body remained in the carriage in front of one of the palaces during that time. To hide the smell of the corpse, dead fish were put next to the body. Six weeks later, Ch'in's body was finally put in the great mausoleum. But his soul had stood before God, the Creator God he had denied, the moment he died.

Food for thought

1. There was no local minister or church during his lifetime; neither, as far as we know, did any prophet of God ever confront Ch'in with his evil ways. Read Romans 1:18–20. Did Ch'in have any excuse?

2. There are many pages of history to which we have little or no access. But God is remembering his children in China today, estimated to number between 6 and 10 percent of its population of over a billion; that is, some 75 million people. The Chinese church is one of the fastest growing in the world, and it is estimated that by the year 2050, the church in China will number well over 100 million believers. All this in spite of the fact that children under the age of eighteen may not be evangelized, all churches must be registered, Christians may not meet in unregistered centres of worship and Christians are not allowed to evangelize outside their churches. There is much persecution by the Communist regime. Comment.

68

Matthew 6:5 *And when you pray, you must not be like the hypocrites. For they love to stand and pray in the synagogues and at the street corners, that they may be seen by others.*

Putting your money where your mouth is

During the Great War, also known as the First World War, many men served in the trenches from 1914 to 1918. It was a horrible way to fight. Day in and day out they faced the dirt, the fear, the waiting, the bullets and the boredom. In the end there were countless dead; there were fields littered with bodies and graves; and there were those who returned battle-scarred and wounded.

This story is about an English regiment during the Great War—a regiment called the Worcester Regiment. The colonel in charge of this particular regiment, which was situated in close proximity to the front-line trenches, had a rather unique sense of humour. He was informed one day that two members of Parliament were coming to "visit" his company. He was also told that these two men were in search of some bravado, some tales which they could relay home. In other words, they wanted to watch some action in which they themselves would not partake, but which would titillate their senses and make them heroes of some sort.

Initially the colonel was extremely miffed to be saddled with such a request. In actuality, he was outraged that such a request could be made. He saw the slime, the dirt, the danger and the fear his men had to contend with on a daily basis, and he was disgusted. But then he had an idea.

When the two members of Parliament were shown to the trenches where the Worcester Regiment was situated, they were told by the colonel that they had arrived at a very crucial and dangerous moment in time.

"There has just been an attack," the colonel informed them in a grave voice, "and we are defending our position vigorously. However, we are heavily outnumbered. The odds are against us, and I should be very surprised if we, and that includes yourselves, escape with our lives."

The two men blanched visibly and asked what they should do.

"Sit here," the colonel told them, pointing to the ground, "against the wall of the trench and do not move. Whatever you do, don't move. Make no noise whatsoever and be very, very quiet."

The two men immediately dropped down. They literally slid to the floor in their good clothes. They said nothing but were very pale and silent. A great racket had erupted even as the colonel was speaking to them. Things were exploding and the line of men who were standing in front of them began firing their guns and throwing hand-grenades with tremendous zeal. Every few moments, a man either to their right or to their left fell down, only to be picked up immediately by stretcher-bearers who appeared out of nowhere. These men were carried away down the trench to a dressing-station. Much to the men's amazement, the stretcher-bearers, as well as the wounded men, were uncommonly cheerful, often whistling as they were carried past them. And as the men fell, others quickly took their place. It was an altogether most heroic and gratifying, if not fearsome, sight.

The entire battle lasted some twenty minutes, although to the two silent and nervous spectators it seemed interminably longer. At the end, when the fire was dying down, the colonel came back to the two men.

"It's all right, gentlemen," he said, "You may stand up now. The attack has been repulsed, and we have overcome."

The men stood up, tremendously relieved. They commented on the valour and cheerfulness of the soldiers.

"What impressed me the most," said one, as he was dusting off his pants, "was the singing and the joy of the men as they were carried off on the stretchers. Although," he added, "I believe that I should have done the same. Yes, indeed, I feel that I was part of them and that I did do it."

The colonel smiled, looked at the well-dressed men in front of him, and stifled a grin behind his hand.

"Ah," he answered, "to be sure, the wounded men are glad to be going home even as you are going home."

"Yes," agreed the gentlemen, on fire with their own perceived boldness, "absolutely."

The two Members of Parliament went back to London determined to speak of their own bravery as well as the bravery of the men in the trenches. They had, in retrospect, thoroughly enjoyed their perceived stint of danger, and were about to bask in the glory of "having been there." They hadn't, however, enjoyed themselves quite as much as the Worcester Regiment—men who had fought a mock battle for the benefit of their smooth-tongued spectators. The battle had been fought, not in the front-line trenches as the two had supposed, but in support trenches some two miles back. The soldiers chuckled over it for a good month after the visit.

Food for thought

1. People are quick to note hypocrisy, whether that hypocrisy is in a Christian or a non-Christian. Although it is true that people's opinions are not crucial in the long run, there is Someone whose opinion of

hypocrisy is crucial. Who is that Someone and why is his opinion crucial?

2. What does this text in Isaiah 29:13 mean: "this people draw near with their mouth and honor me with their lips, while their hearts are far from me"? Must you always do what you say? Why or why not?

69

Deuteronomy 5:16 *Honor your father and your mother, as the Lord your God commanded you; that your days may be long, and that it may go well with you in the land that the Lord your God is giving you.*

With a promise

This Jewish folk tale is about a father who had three sons. The oldest son and the youngest boy prospered and became wealthy, but the middle child did not do very well. Indeed, he lived in poverty and had to struggle to make ends meet.

One day, many years after they had left home, the oldest son received a letter from his father telling him that the youngest sibling was getting married and that the wedding was to take place shortly. The letter read, in part:

Son, please come home and be sure to bring with you your younger brother so that we may all celebrate together at the wedding. I promise to pay all the travelling expenses that you may incur in fulfilling the commandment, 'Honour thy father and thy mother.'

The oldest son read the letter to his wife and children and together they went on a shopping spree. They bought themselves costly materials and had dressmakers sew the materials into rich gowns and suits. They preened and pranced about before mirrors and did not even waste one moment of thought on the middle brother. They had had very little contact with him, and they did not even inform him about the wedding. As the day of departure for the ancestral home dawned, however, the oldest brother did recall that he had been asked to bring his impoverished sibling along. Consequently, he had a servant call around to tell him to come immediately. The poor fellow came and was told to step inside the carriage. Upon his entrance, the horses took off at great speed.

"Why did you ask me to come? Where are we going?"

The middle son, pushed into the corner of the carriage by his older brother, was bewildered, and when he was tersely told their destination, he fingered his threadbare clothes with shame. Many people were watching as the great carriage stopped in front of the father's house. When the oldest son alighted in all his finery, many people ooh'd and ah'd. But when the younger son stepped out clad in his rags, people shook their heads and turned away.

The wedding was celebrated with much merriment. There was fine food, dancing, singing and gaiety, and the bride and groom were sweet to behold.

After some days had passed in this fashion, the older son went to the father and said, "Father, I have obeyed you and have come to celebrate at this wedding feast of my younger brother. I rejoiced with you and the couple, but now I have to go back home. As you know, I'm a merchant and my business can't prosper when I'm not in town."

"Do what you think is best, my son," the father answered.

The son packed his things and gathered up his family, but his heart was overflowing with hidden anger. Shouldn't his father have confirmed by this time that he was ready to pay for the clothes he had bought for himself and his wife and children? Shouldn't he have sat down with him to tabulate all the expenses he had drawn up travelling all this way? Irritated beyond words, he sat down at his dressing table and itemized all the bills on a piece of paper. This paper he handed to his father on his way out.

"What's this, son? Bills for clothes, bills for inns and bills for fodder for the horses?"

"Yes," the son said, his resentment increasing by the minute, "and did you not promise to repay me for all my expenses if I came to the wedding?"

The father looked at the son in mild astonishment.

"I did not make any such promise," he said firmly.

The eldest son reached into his coat pocket and drew out the letter which his father had written to him and read the pertinent sentence out loud.

"I promise to pay all the travelling expenses that you may incur in fulfilling the commandment, 'Honour thy father and thy mother.'"

Then he stood quietly in front of his father, staring at him in a forceful manner before continuing in a demanding voice.

"So what have you to say now, father? Did you promise or did you not promise?"

"Well," said his father, steadily returning his oldest son's gaze as he answered, "let us just go over carefully what exactly I wrote to you. I promised to reimburse you for all the expenses that you would incur in the fulfilment of the commandment, 'Honour thy father and thy mother.'"

The son nodded and the father went on.

"Had you really wished to honour me you would have taken pity on your poor brother and you would have clothed him suitably when you brought him with you. You would have understood that to honour me was to clothe him decently and to help him. So, you see, the expenses you incurred for the wedding were only for your own honour. And for your own honour, son, I did not promise to pay."

Food for thought

1. Proverbs 10:27 reiterates the command and blessing of Deuteronomy 5:16: "The fear of the Lord prolongs life, but the years of the wicked will be short." What are parents actually doing when they refuse to chastise their children?

2. It is easier not to punish and to let a child have his or her own way. Comment.

70

Proverbs 31:10–11, 23 *An excellent wife who can find? She is far more precious than jewels. The heart of her husband trusts in her, and he will have no lack of gain.... Her husband is known in the gates when he sits among the elders of the land.*

Sophie's strength
PART 1

Sophie Elisabeth Bonicel was born in Nimes, France, in 1765, the first of fifteen children. Her parents brought her up to worship and honour the Lord. As a young girl, Sophie was extremely conscious of her love for God and also of the love her parents demonstrated for one another. Therefore, she made a commitment in her youth only to marry for both of these loves. God honoured Sophie's godly requirements. Before she was twenty-one, she had met André Guizot, an able, up-and-coming young advocate whose father was a Huguenot pastor. A godly man, he captured her heart with both his eloquence and his conduct. They were married in 1786, on the eve of the French Revolution.

Over the next few years, André became established as a distinguished and honest lawyer. Outspoken in disagreement with the politics of the guillotine and the rampant execution of many innocent citizens, his life was constantly in danger. The Reign of Terror had begun. Together with Sophie and their two children, André fled Paris back to his estate in Nimes.

André hid for four months in Nimes. For several weeks, he was a fugitive, fleeing from one place to another in the hill country of Southern France, protected by a number of loyal friends. Sophie and the children had been brought to safety on her father's estate. Eventually, however, André was caught—caught by a *gendarme* who had known and respected him for many years. The *gendarme* was very upset.

"Shall I let you escape?" said the *gendarme*.

"Are you married?" André replied.

"Yes," responded the *gendarme*, "and I have two children."

"And so have I," André said softly, "but you would have to pay for me—don't be afraid to arrest me, my good fellow. Let us go on to the authorities."

Back in Paris, André was rapidly brought to trial. He appeared fearlessly before many men with whom he had worked only a year or so before.

"You yourselves," he said, as he stood in the prisoner's dock, "will have to appear before the judgement seat of God even as I will. But I do not fear him. Do you?"

A number of the judges squirmed, and consequently his case was pushed through rapidly. They did not like having a conscience stand before them. André was condemned to death and taken from their sight.

Sophie was ill at this time. She had travelled back to Paris with the boys to do what she could to aid in her husband's release. But try as she might, she could not rise from her bed. The two boys, Francois, who was now six and a half years old, and Jean, who was four and a half, were taken by a servant to say goodbye to their father at the House of Justice. A great many people had been thrown together in a large cell—all of them were richly dressed and most of them distraught. Gentlemen walked about with their wigs askew and fine ladies, whose rustling silk skirts were soiled with dirt, stood in small groups. A terrible stench pervaded the cell. Everyone approached the little boys. Everyone wanted the tiny lads to carry a note; to take a message; and to deliver some token to someone somewhere. But André took his sons to a corner, put his arms about them and hugged them.

"My sons," he then said, "my fine, strong sons."

For a moment his voice faltered but then he continued.

"You must always stand for truth. Serve God with all your heart and soul and mind."

Francois nodded gravely.

"Take care of your mother, Francois," André went on, "obey her in all things. She will be your guardian from now on."

The boy nodded again, his face white, but his round childish chin jutted out resolutely.

"I will, Father," he managed to whisper, "I will."

Jean began to whimper, and Francois took his hand. André put his hand into his vest and drew out a paper.

"A letter for your mother," he said, "take care she receives it, son."

Francois nodded again, took the paper, solemnly hiding the writing behind his vest even as he smiled at his father. They left soon afterward, Francois looking back over his shoulder at his father a number of times. André was guillotined the next day.

Food for thought

1. What qualities about André helped Sophie in her decision to marry him? Why are these biblical qualities?

2. Do godly qualities often come with a price? Explain.

71

Sophie's strength
PART 2

The letter for Sophie that André had sent along with his son from prison, has been preserved.

My very dear Sophie,
These are, I have no doubt, the very last words which I will speak to you this side of heaven. I would I might kiss you once more, but am convinced the Lord will bear you up as with eagle's wings. His embrace is a thousand times better than mine. Please do so promise me, my dear wife, that you will live for our children. You must now supply my

place alongside your own. Give all your energy to this task and surely God shall help you. Daily implore our heavenly Father to guard them....as for me, I do not fear and live in the sure knowledge that before the week is out I shall see my Saviour face to face.... You have been a fine wife to me and I beg your forgiveness for aught I might have wronged you with. My love has not done you justice. Oh, to hold you once more...oh, to see your dear face one more time.... Adieu, my beloved, until we meet again.
André Francois Guizot, 1794.

The letter André so tenderly and passionately penned in prison, was kept by Sophie—she carried it close to her heart until the day she died. André's estates were confiscated when he was arrested but they were restored a year and a half later. Sophie and the boys lived with her father for a while but, in 1799, she moved to Geneva, where both Francois and Jean were educated. It was a big step for a widow to make on her own. Francois was eleven at the time.

In the beginning, Sophie was present at all the boys' lessons and studied with them. Sometimes in the winter, in the small house they had rented, the temperature was so cold that the children's hands were inflamed, and Sophie would have to write out their dictation.

The money from André's estate dwindled, and life was not easy. Sophie, however, was determined that the boys should learn from lectures by godly professors. She also made both of them learn a trade. She was constant in leading them in daily devotions and never ceased to pray for her sons.

Sophie Guizot died at a good old age and was buried as a godly mother who lived in the sure hope of the resurrection. By the grace of God, she had been able to teach sure principles and firm foundations.

Food for thought

1. What was the strength that enabled Sophie to bring up her sons? If

all parents relied on the strength Sophie had, do you think there would be a revival within the church? Why or why not?

2. It is interesting to read of the subsequent life of Sophie's son, Francois. After studying in Geneva, he initially became a journalist. In 1812, he became a professor of modern history at the Sorbonne and wrote some monumental works of history. After 1814, he became involved in politics and held posts in the government, first as minister of foreign affairs and later as prime minister of France. Although he passed through a period of skepticism and denied predestination, toward the end of his life he returned to the faith of his youth, and he became an administrator in the French Protestant church. How important in a child's life is the initial teaching of a parent?

72

2 Timothy 4:1–4 *I charge you in the presence of God and of Christ Jesus who is to judge the living and the dead, and by his appearing and his kingdom: preach the word; be ready in season and out of season; reprove, rebuke, and exhort, with complete patience and teaching. For the time is coming when people will not endure sound teaching, but having itching ears they will accumulate for themselves teachers to suit their own passions, and will turn away from listening to the truth and wander off into myths.*

Itching ears

On July 8, 1971, a news report alerted the world that a small tribe of "Stone Age" natives had been discovered deep in the rainforest of Mindanao, the second largest island of the Philippines. These natives, it was reported, were still living in caves, as indeed, they had done for thousands of years. The tribe was called Tasaday. Unaware of the modern world, they lived secluded in the rainforest, never setting foot outside their small area of living. Using bamboo slivers for knives, and stones tied to bamboo handles for hammers, they represented the quintessential cave people. They ate what the area provided—grubs, wild fruit, yams and a few other things—and used no traps or hunting devices.

The modern world was quite overcome. This was exciting news. Surely many unanswered questions concerning evolution could be learned from these people. Anthropologists and paleontologists eagerly anticipated visiting the Tasaday. This was a fantastic opportunity to study paleolithic man as he had been for thousands of years.

Within days, the Mindanao airport was a busy place—an extremely busy place. NBC, *National Geographic*, *Life* magazine, and *The New York Times* were only a few of the big names that could be seen lugging cameras, notebooks and pencils past airport hangars. Enthusiasm was somewhat curbed, however, when it was found out that the rainforest was more difficult to access than Disney World. The Tasaday caves were located in one of the most dense and uncharted parts of the rainforest. Laborious travel over hundreds of miles of mountainous terrain, followed by hacking one's way through thick jungle, was called for. Those who did, by sheer perseverance, manage to make it to the edge of the rainforest, were confronted by a man with the name of Manuel Elizalde.

Manuel Elizalde was chief of the Philippine's department for national minorities. He was also the man who had made the news release about the Tasaday tribe. He told the people who had made it as far as they did, that he was not about to permit them to continue because he was afraid that too large an infiltration of people would probably destroy the Tasaday. However, he was willing to compromise.

Elizalde's compromise involved money—a lot of money. Any poor freelancer without access to finances was at the end of the line at this point. Elizalde made travel arrangements only for those who could pay him. He allowed them passage on his personal helicopter and flew them directly to the site where the Tasaday lived. Lowered onto the rainforest floor, the people who were fortunate enough to have made it this far were immediately embraced by the small tribe of some twenty-five members. Scientists and journalists alike were charmed.

The Tasadays appeared to be a friendly people. They offered their food to the newcomers; they shared their cave beds; in short, they treated everyone as family. In a relatively small period of time, they began to mimic Western speech and even played with the radio equipment.

It was found that the Tasaday practiced no religion, performed no marriages and kept no cemeteries. (Dead bodies, the visitors were told, were left in the forest under layers of leaves.) Their ancestors had prophesied that a Good Man would come, bringing them joy. They thought this man was Elizalde.

There was a fountain of news about the community. Magazines wrote up articles speaking of harmony, innocence and peace. Photographs featuring naked cave-people cuddling wide-eyed children, captured the hearts of many. CBS featured a *National Geographic* special on the *Last Tribes of Mindanao*. President Marcos of the Philippines designated 70,000 hectares of the rainforest as a reservation area. An organized American Tasaday fund was created. The Smithsonian Institute invited Elizalde to Washington. Reports and studies were funded, written and read by a growing number of academics and scientists. And the money kept pouring in.

It was not until 1986, some fifteen years after the first report of the Tasaday surfaced, that a Swiss journalist made it to the tribe without guides. He discovered that the tribe was not at home. The caves were uninhabited and the area was clean. There was no garbage, no sign of the fact that anyone had lived in the rainforest for some time. The journalist travelled on and stayed in one of the villages on the edge of the rainforest. Here the natives made him aware of the fact that the Tasaday often left their area and visited them, buying food at their markets to augment their diet.

Investigation, which followed soon after the Swiss journalist wrote up a rather incriminating report, found the "Stone Age" Tasaday cavemen to be living in ordinary huts in proximity of the rainforest. They were seen to be wearing T-shirts and jeans, smoking cigarettes and wearing watches. As a matter of fact, the whole set-up had been concocted by Elizalde to attract foreign aid and government protection for the area. "Elizalde said we would get help if we went around naked," the would-be cave dwellers said, "but he lied. We're poorer now than we were before."

Elizalde not only lied, he disappeared. In the confusion that ensued when the government of dictator Ferdinand Marcos fell, he fled the country. He did not flee empty-handed. He took $241 million with him—money that had been donated by itching ears.

Food for thought

1. Someone once said to Charles Spurgeon, "How can you admire this man? You don't believe what he says." "No," answered Spurgeon, "but he does." The point being that an earnest person can persuade beautifully. What kind of people do you believe and why?

2. There are foolish teachers, but there are also foolish listeners. What category do people fall into who deny the Bible is the actual, infallible Word of God? What category do you fall into and why?

73

Hebrews 11:32–40 *And what more shall I say? For time would fail me to tell of Gideon, Barak, Samson, Jepthah, of David and Samuel and the prophets—who through faith conquered kingdoms, enforced justice, obtained promises, stopped the mouths of lions, quenched the power of fire, escaped the edge of the sword, were made strong out of weakness, became mighty in war, put foreign armies to flight. Women received back their dead by resurrection. Some were tortured, refusing to accept release, so that they might rise again to a better life. Others suffered mocking and flogging, and even chains and imprisonment. They were stoned, they were sawn in two, they were killed with the sword...all these, though commended through their faith, did not receive what was promised, since God had provided something better for us, that apart from us they should not be made perfect.*

Khamara's faith

A story was related by the Romanian pastor Richard Wurmbrandt (1909–2001), about a Russian man named Nikolai Khamara. Khamara was an atheist. That is to say, he did not believe in God, but in himself. He thought himself number one and tried to make sure that he got the best of things. Taking freely what did not belong to him, he lived high. However, his life of crime was discovered. Caught by the police, Khamara was charged with robbery. A judge sentenced him to ten years imprisonment.

But "all things work together for good to those who love God and are called according to his purpose" (Romans 8:28). During those ten years, Khamara came into contact with some Christians who had been imprisoned for their faith. Put into cells with these God-fearing people, he told them the story of his life. He confessed that he had stolen and had thought only of himself. They listened and spoke to him of Jesus. But Khamara did not seem to understand what they were saying.

Despairingly, he shouted to them, "I am a lost man!"

One of the Christians took this opportunity to testify to Khamara yet again and said, "What is the value of a ten ruble note if I lose it?"

Khamara grinned and replied, "Ten rubles are ten rubles. You have lost them but the one who has found them is very happy."

"You have answered well," the Christian said. "And now I will ask you another question. Someone loses a gold ring. What is the value of that gold ring when it is lost?"

"That's a foolish question," Khamara said. "A gold ring is a gold ring. You have lost it, but somebody else will have found it."

"Now tell me," the Christian went on, "what is the value of a lost man?"

Khamara looked down and answered nothing and the Christian continued.

"A lost man—such as a thief, or an adulterer, or a murderer—still has the whole value of a man. As a matter of fact, he is of such value that the Son of God forsook heaven for him and died on the cross to save him."

Eventually, as the Holy Spirit worked in his heart, Khamara became a Christian through the testimony of those who were imprisoned with him. He finished his ten-year term and was freed. Thankful to be out of his cell, he breathed deeply and felt a great joy bursting his heart. How vast the sky looked, how beautiful the flowers bloomed and how wonderful to be able to come and go as he pleased. Yet, because he had committed his life to the Lord Jesus, one of the first things he did upon his release was to seek out the underground church in Russia. He became a member and gathered secretly with other believers each week to worship the Lord. The people loved him and accepted him with happiness and

Khamara felt as if he had become a member of a new family.

After a few months, the pastor of Khamara's church was arrested and beaten. The authorities wanted him to tell them who the members of his church were, but the pastor stood firm and would not divulge those names. Aware that their former prisoner Khamara had also become a Christian, the authorities also arrested him and brought him to the same room as the pastor. Then they threatened the pastor that they would torture Khamara if he would not tell them who the other members of the church were. Khamara, seeing how difficult it was for the pastor, encouraged him.

"Be faithful to Christ and do not betray him. I am happy to suffer for the name of Christ."

The pastor did not speak and the cruel interrogators gouged out Khamara's eyes in full view of the pastor.

That poor pastor cried out, "How can I bear this?! You are blind!"

Khamara answered, "Although my eyes have been taken away from me, I see more beauty without them than with them. I see my Saviour. Be faithful to Christ!"

The interrogators then threatened to cut out Khamara's tongue and the last words he spoke to his weeping pastor were, "Praise the Lord Jesus Christ! I have said the best words that could be spoken. And now, if you wish, you can cut out my tongue."

Khamara died a martyr's death.

Food for thought

1. Hebrews 11 is full of people like Khamara—people whose funerals were not functions where bouquets of flowers covered graves, or where people lined the roadside mourning. No, their deaths were miserable and gruesome. Jesus' death was likewise grievous. Isaiah 53:3 says: "He was despised and rejected by men; a man of sorrows and acquainted with grief; and as one from whom men hide their faces he was despised, and we esteemed him not." How can you hide your face from Jesus, and how can you not esteem him?

2. Matthew 16:26 says, "For what will it profit a man, if he gains the

whole world and forfeits his soul? Or what shall a man give in return for his soul?" What is the value of a soul?

74

Mark 16:15 *And he said to them, "Go into all the world and proclaim the gospel to the whole creation."*

Epilogue—Jonah Brown and the Great Commission

A Jonah Brown from York, you say?
Is he perhaps related to
The Jonah Brown from Nineveh?
Ah, now you grin! Probably knew
That Jonah Browns are everywhere,
From Nunavut to Delaware
To South America. They clear
Both of the earth's great hemispheres.
Statistics say and facts construe,
That many vessels have a queue

Of Jonahs anxious to board on,
To leave their calling and be gone.
From Adam to the present day,
There's been desire to sail away.
The answer to why that is so
Lies in the lineage, you know.
And this is not at all that odd,
For all the Jonahs' feet are shod
With sin original—the key
To why they flee away to sea.
You nod and smile, as if to say
You've seen some Jonahs in your day.
But please to understand and know
All middle monikers are Joe.
Like pudding molds within a frame,
Sin sets rebellion on a name.
Sons of Amittai all are we,
Obeying insufficiently;
All Jonah Browns who sink away
Into the belly of our day.
Idols like seaweed round our head
Bar us from life, desire us dead.
Money and power, prestige and fame
Render us drowned, sully God's name.
Yet through Christ's grace, his great command
Vomits our presence on dry land,
And bids us walk our streets with dread,
Leaving no prophecy unsaid.

Food for thought

1. When and where have you ever walked away from a situation where you should have spoken out about God's love and mercy in Jesus Christ?

2. The Great Commission in Mark 16 is addressed to "all those who love the Lord Jesus." How and why are you fulfilling it?

Deo Optimo et Maximo Gloria
To God, best and greatest, be glory

www.joshuapress.com

CPSIA information can be obtained
at www.ICGtesting.com
Printed in the USA
FFOW02n0436140416
23134FF